NUTCASES

EUROPEAN UNION LAW

D1347267

AUSTRALIA
Law Book Company
Sydney

CANADA and USA
Carswell
Toronto

HONG KONG
Sweet & Maxwell Asia

NEW ZEALAND
Brookers
Wellington

SINGAPORE and MALAYSIA
Sweet & Maxwell Asia
Singapore and Kuala Lumpur

NUTCASES

EUROPEAN UNION LAW

FOURTH EDITION

by

PENELOPE KENT
LLB, LLM Solicitor
Principal Lecturer
Middlesex Business School
Middlesex University

London ● Sweet & Maxwell ● 2006

First Edition 1997
Reprinted 1999
Second Edition 2000
Reprinted 2002
Third Edition 2003
Fourth Edition 2006

Published in 2006 by Sweet & Maxwell Limited of
100 Avenue Road,
London NW3 3PF
www.sweetandmaxwell.co.uk

Computerised by LBJ Typesetting Ltd of Kingsclere
Printed in Great Britain by
Creative Print and Design (Wales) Ebbw Vale

No natural forests were destroyed to make this product.
only farmed timber was used and replanted.

A CIP catalogue record for this book is available from the
British Library.

ISBN 0421928603

CONTENTS

TABLE OF CASES

TABLE OF ABBREVIATIONS

CAP	Common Agricultural Policy
CCT	Common Customs Tariff
CET	Common External Tariff
CFI	Court of First Instance
CMLR	Common Market Law Reports
EC	European Community/Communities
ECA	European Community Act 1972
ECB	European Central Bank
ECHR	European Convention for the Protection of Human Rights and Fundamental Freedoms
ECJ	European Court of Justice
ECR	European Court Reports
ECSC	European Coal and Steel Community
EEA	European Economic Area
EEC	European Economic Community
EETA	European Free Trade Association
EMU	European Monetary Union
EP	European Parliament
EPU	European Political Union
EU	European Union
EURATOM	European Atomic Energy Authority
IGC	Intergovernmental Conference
O.J.	Official Journal
SEA	Single European Act
TEU	Treaty on European Union
TN	Treaty of Nice
TOA	Treaty of Amsterdam

1. LEGAL ORDER OF THE EC AND EU

Introduction

The present European Community (EC) and European Union (EU) originated in the European Economic Community (EEC), created in 1957 by the Treaty of Rome (EEC Treaty). The Treaty provided for a customs union and a common market (the free movement of goods, persons, services and capital) for the six signatory states (Germany, France, Italy, Belgium, the Netherlands and Luxembourg). These states also created the European Coal and Steel Community (ECSC) and the European Atomic Energy Authority (Euratom). The United Kingdom, Denmark and Ireland joined in 1973. The United Kingdom enacted the European Communities Act (ECA 1972) in 1972 to give effect to its obligations under EC law. Further accessions took place in 1981 (Greece), 1986 (Spain and Portugal) and 1995 (Austria, Sweden and Finland).

There are five main institutions which are entrusted with carrying out the tasks of the community: the Council of Ministers (an ad hoc body of ministers from the Member States responsible for the adoption of legislation); the Commission (a permanent body which proposes legislation and monitors the implementation of EC law); the European Parliament (EP) (directly elected since 1979 but with only a limited role in the legislative process) the Court of Justice (the final authority on matters of EC law, now assisted by the Court of First Instance) and the Court of Auditors.

The EEC Treaty was amended in 1986 by the Single European Act (SEA), in 1993 by the Treaty on European Union (TEU or the Maastricht Treaty), after which it was known as the EC Treaty, and in 1997 by the Treaty of Amsterdam (ToA). The SEA provided the mechanism to complete the single or internal market, an area without internal frontiers within which goods, persons, services and capital may circulate freely. The TEU created a three-pillar structure. After amendment by the ToA, the three pillars are as follows:

[i] the EC (i.e. the ECSC, Euratom and the EC, as the EEC was renamed);

[ii] the Common Foreign and Security Policy; and

[iii] Police and Judicial Co-operation (previously, under the Maastricht Treaty, Co-operation in Justice and Home Affairs).

The first pillar, the EC, is governed by law under the EC Treaty, whereas the second and third pillars are administered through intergovernmental co-operation. The Maastricht Treaty provided for both political (EPU) and monetary union (EMU). The United Kingdom, through protocols annexed to the Treaty "opted out" of EMU and, at the time of the Maastricht Treaty, of the Agreement on Social Policy (the Social Chapter) which established a legal base for certain forms of employment protection.

The changes introduced by the Maastricht Treaty were reviewed in an Intergovernmental Conference (IGC) from 1996 to 1997, leading to the finalisation of the Amsterdam Treaty (ToA) in June 1997. Ratification by all Member States was completed on May 1, 1999, the date on which the Treaty amendments came into force. The ToA introduced into the Treaty an Employment Chapter, requiring Member States to co-ordinate their economic policies, focusing on growth and employment. Inclusion of the Employment Chapter may be seen by some as a move towards greater recognition of the social dimension. The ToA had no effect on EMU, the third stage of which began on January 1, 1999 when the single currency came into operation in the participating states.

The ECJ now has jurisdiction in certain areas relating to Police and Judicial Co-operation (the third pillar). The Social Chapter was incorporated into the body of the revised Treaty, following the change of government in the United Kingdom. Article 13 of the Treaty provides a basis for action to combat discrimination on grounds of gender, race, religion, sexual orientation, or disability. Sanctions may be imposed on Member States for human rights infringements. Two Directives were adopted in 2000 under Art.13, the first on equal treatment irrespective of racial or ethnic origins and the second to provide a general framework for equal treatment in employment and occupation.

The Schengen Agreement, by which participating states agreed to relax border formalities on the movement of people, was incorporated in the revised Treaty. The United Kingdom and Ireland have "opted out" of this part of the treaty; Denmark has obtained various exemptions. The European leaders at

Amsterdam were unable to agree on institutional reforms, a major issue which it had been hoped would be resolved before the admission of any new Member States. The ToA was reviewed at an IGC between February and December 2000. This process culminated in the signing of the Treaty of Nice (TN) in February 2001, with the Treaty coming into force on February 1, 2003.

The TN prepared the way for substantial further enlargement of the EU to take in a large number of mainly Eastern European states. With a near-doubling of members, the new EU has become a very different body from the existing one. As a result, major changes will be required; particularly in the structure and composition of the institutions. The TN limits itself to setting out principles and methods to change the system as the EU expands, seen in the Protocol on Enlargement and other documents. Changes to the composition of the Commission and weighted voting in the Council applied from 2005, whereas changes to the number of MEPs applied from the elections in 2004. The arrangements for new applicants joining before these dates were determined by the terms of the accession treaty.

In December 2001, the Laeken European Council issued a Declaration leading to the setting up of the European Convention, a process involving existing Member States and applicant states in discussion over the future direction of the EU. The Convention on the Future of Europe opened in March 2002 under the Chairmanship of Giscard d'Estaing, the former French President and closed in March 2003. The draft Treaty presented by the Convention to the Thessaloniki European Council in June 2003 was rejected, due to continuing differences over qualified majority voting in the Council.

Enlargement of the EU took place on May 1, 2004, resulting in the addition of 10 new Member States (the Czech Republic, Estonia, Cyprus, Latvia, Lithuania, Hungary, Malta, Poland, Slovenia and Slovakia). In the absence of a new Treaty, institutional changes were governed by the provisions of the various acts of accession and the Treaty of Nice.

Agreement was eventually reached on a Constitutional Treaty for the EU, which was signed in Rome in October 2004. The Treaty will not, however, become binding until it has been ratified by all 25 Member States. Negative results in referenda on the Treaty held in France and the Netherlands in May and June 2005 have cast doubt on the whole process of ratification. While the Treaty has not been abandoned, it is impossible to say when, or even if, it will be fully ratified. It could be argued that the rejection of the Treaty in two Member States reflects a wider dissatisfaction with the institutions of the EU among its citizens. Unless these citizens can identify with the objectives and commitments of the Treaty, they are unlikely to give the ratification process their support.

If the ratification process is completed, the Constitutional Treaty will make a number of changes. These include the fusion of the three pillars introduced by the Maastricht Treaty into a single entity, namely the European Union. The Treaty will incorporate the Charter of Fundamental Rights into the body of the Treaty. Specific provision is made for the primacy of EU law over national law, reflecting the principles developed by the Court of Justice through its case law. Further changes will be made to the institutions, including the number of commissioners and the weighting of qualified majority voting. Clarification is provided on the division of competence between the EU and the Member States.

It should be noted that the ToA renumbered the Articles of the EC Treaty, as part of a process of simplification resulting from the amendment and repeal of many Articles. To avoid confusion, the new numbering is used throughout the book, although, strictly speaking, it was operative only from May 1, 1999. The first time a Treaty Article is cited, both forms of numbering are given, first the new numbering, followed by the old number in brackets with the prefix "ex": see, for example, Art.28 (ex 30).

The new legal order

Key Principle: **The objective of the EC is to establish a common market, the operation of which directly concerns interested parties in the Community.**

Van Gend en Loos v Nederlandse Administratie der Belastinge (Case 26/62) 1963
Van Gend en Loos, a firm of importers, was required to pay customs duty on urea-formaldehyde (glue) imported from Germany into the Netherlands under a law adopted after the creation of the EEC. The importers challenged the payment in the Dutch courts on the basis that the extra duty infringed Art.25 (ex 12) of the Treaty (prohibiting the introduction of new customs duties). The Dutch court referred questions to the Court

of Justice (ECJ) for interpretation under Art.234 (ex 177) procedure.

Held: (ECJ) (1) The EC (then known as the EEC) is a new legal order in international law, on behalf of which states have limited their sovereign rights in certain fields and whose subjects comprise not only states but also individuals; (2) Art.25 (ex 12) of the Treaty produces direct effects in the relationship between the Member States and their subjects, creating individual rights which national courts must protect. [1963] E.C.R. 1.

Commentary

The "new legal order" is recognised in international law as a treaty between sovereign states but also takes effect within the domestic legal systems of the Member States. The order is characterised by the concepts of direct effect and the supremacy of EC law over national law. Where a provision of EC law is directly effective it creates rights and duties which are directly enforceable by individuals before the national courts. The ECJ stated in *Van Gend en Loos* that to create direct effects a provision must be clear, unconditional and require no further action by Member States.

Supremacy and direct effect

Key Principle: **The EC Treaty is an integral part of the legal system of the Member States and must be applied in their courts.**

Costa v ENEL (Case 6/64) 1964

Ente Nazional Energia Elettrica (ENEL) was created by the Italian Government under a law passed in 1962 to nationalise the electricity industry. Costa refused to pay his electricity bill, on the basis that the nationalisation infringed the Italian Constitution and various provisions of the Treaty.

Held: (ECJ) The transfer by Member States from their domestic legal systems to the EC system of rights and duties carries with it a permanent limitation of their sovereign rights, against which a later, unilateral act incompatible with EC law cannot prevail. [1964] E.C.R. 585.

Italian Minister of Finance v Simmenthal (Case 106/77) 1978

An Italian law introduced after joining the EEC required veterinary inspections of beef and veal. The law was challenged before the Italian courts as contrary to Art.28 (ex 30) (prohibiting quantitative restrictions on imports and measures having equivalent effect).

Held: (ECJ) A national court in such circumstances should not apply conflicting national legislation, even in situations where it was adopted after joining the EEC; it should not wait for the decision of a higher national court before acting. [1978] E.C.R. 629.

The Constitutional Treaty provides for the supremacy of Community law over national law in as follows: 'The Constitution and laws adopted by the institutions of the Union in exercising competences conferred on it shall have primacy over the law of the Member States' (Article 1–6).

Commentary

The ECJ recently reconsidered *Simmenthal* in *Ministero della Finanze v In.Co.Ge.90* (Joined Cases C-10-22/97) 1998, holding that it does not follow from *Simmenthal* that the conflicting national law should be regarded as non-existent. The Court held that where a national law is adopted after an EC law with which it is incompatible, it is for the national authorities to decide on its reclassification.

The Art.234 (ex 177) procedure enables the ECJ to interpret or consider the validity of EC law (see Ch.7). The ECJ has used this procedure to develop the concept of the "new legal order" and to provide authoritative rulings, which apply uniformly throughout all the Member States. The United Kingdom recognised the direct effect of EC law in s.2(1) of the European Communities Act 1972.

Interim relief

Key Principle: **The full effectiveness of EC law would be impaired if a rule of national law could prevent a court considering a matter governed by EC law from granting interim relief.**

R. v Secretary of State for Transport Ex p. Factortame (Case C-213/89) 1990
Following concern about the tenuous nature of the link between the owners of a number of fishing vessels and the United Kingdom, the Merchant Shipping Act 1988 was adopted, setting out stringent rules for the registration of fishing vessels as

British. Many vessels owned by Spanish nationals previously registered as British no longer qualified and thus could not share in the United Kingdom fishing quota under the common fisheries policy. The unsuccessful applicants sought judicial review in the United Kingdom and suspension of the relevant parts of the 1988 Act, arguing that the Act contravened various provisions of the Treaty. An injunction against the Secretary of State was refused. The House of Lords referred questions for interpretation to the ECJ under Art.234 (ex 177).

Held: (ECJ) A national law should be set aside where it prevents the granting of interim relief in a dispute governed by EC law. [1990] E.C.R. I-2433.

Commentary
The ruling of the ECJ followed the interim decision of the same court in an enforcement action brought by the Commission against the United Kingdom under Art.226 (ex 69): *Commission v UK* (Case C-246/89R), ordering the United Kingdom to suspend the operation of the offending sections of the 1988 Act. The House of Lords applied the decision and set aside the rule that an interim injunction cannot be granted against the Crown in *R. v Secretary of State for Transport Ex p. Factortame* (1991). The ECJ later ruled on the interpretation of the substantive provisions of the Treaty (in Case C-221/89R), holding that Arts 43 (ex 52), etc., were infringed in circumstances where registration was made more difficult for nationals from other Member States than for nationals from the host state.

The direct effect of regulations, directives and decisions

Key Principle: Regulations, directives and decisions are capable of creating direct effects.

Grad v Finanzamt Traunstein (Case 9/70) 1970
A haulage contractor challenged a German transport tax on the basis that it infringed a decision addressed to the Member States on VAT and a harmonisation directive imposing a deadline for implementation of the decision.

Held: (ECJ) (1) The wording of Art.249 (ex 189) does not prevent individuals from relying in the national courts on decisions addressed to Member States. (2) The decision was directly effective; the directive merely fixed the date on which the VAT regime in the decision took effect. [1970] E.C.R. 825.

Commentary
The ECJ adopted the same reasoning in *Van Duyn v Home Office* (Case 41/74), holding that directives can be directly effective. Regulations are stated in Art.189 to be "of general application". If they are also clear and unconditional, they may be directly effective: *Leonesio v Italian Ministry of Agriculture* (Case 93/71).

Key Principle: **A directive containing a deadline for implementation is only capable of creating direct effects from the date of the deadline.**

Pubblico Ministero v Ratti (Case 148/78) 1979
Ratti, a manufacturer of solvents in Italy, was charged with failure to comply with Italian labelling legislation. He claimed that his products were labelled according to EC standards contained in two directives.

Held: (ECJ) As the deadline for implementation had been reached in relation to one but not both of the directives, only the directive for which the deadline had expired could be relied upon to create direct effects (and thus to provide a defence to one of the criminal charges). [1972] E.C.R. 119.

Commentary
If no deadline is specified in a directive it takes effect on publication in the Official Journal.

Vertical and horizontal direct effects

Key Principle: **Treaty provisions are capable of creating direct effects both vertically between the state and individuals and horizontally between individuals.**

Defrenne v Sabena (Case 43/75) 1976
Ms D, an airline stewardess employed by the Belgian airline Sabena, was paid less and had to retire earlier than male

stewards. She claimed that this amounted to a breach of Art.119 (now 141) of the Treaty (providing for equal pay for equal work).

Held: (Under Art.234 (ex 177)) Art.119 creates direct effects both vertically and horizontally. [1976] E.C.R. 4545.

Commentary
The ruling in *Defrenne* was limited to Treaty provisions. Article 119 was treated as directly effective only from the date of the judgment. This ruling on temporal effect was unusual but not unique and was based on the need for legal certainty. See also *Barber v Guardian Royal* Exchange (Case C-262/88) (Ch.14, p.175).

Key Principle: **Directives are capable of creating direct effects vertically but not horizontally.**

Marshall v South West Area Health Authority (No.1) (Case 152/84) 1986
Ms M sought to rely on Art.5 of the Equal Treatment Directive 76/207 when she was required to retire at 60 when men did not have to retire until the age of 65. The House of Lords referred questions to the ECJ.

Held: (ECJ) (1) Differentiating between retirement ages for men and women contravenes Art.5 of the Directive. (2) The obligation in a directive is addressed to Member States and cannot be enforced against individuals. (3) As an area health authority is a public body, the obligation not to discriminate may be enforced directly against that body. [1986] E.C.R. 723.

Commentary

(1) *Marshall* established for the first time that directives could not be enforced directly against individuals, unless the individual is a public body (or "emanation of the state").

(2) In *Foster v British Gas* (Case C-188/89) the ECJ held that a directive could be enforced against a body responsible for providing a public service under state control, possessing special powers greater than those normally applicable

between individuals (e.g. privatised utilities such as gas, water and electricity). In *NUT v St Mary's Church of England Junior School* the Court of Appeal held that the governors of a church school were a public body as they were charged by the state with running the school.

(3) The limitation on the direct effect of directives was upheld in *Faccini Dori v Recreb* (Case C-91/92). (Ms FD could not rely on the cooling-off period in a consumer protection directive against an Italian company when she sought to cancel a contract for a language course entered into on Milan Station.)

(4) The lack of horizontal direct effect in directives was again confirmed in El Corte Ingles SA v Rivero (Case C-192/94). In this case it was held that Art.153 (ex 129a) EC (providing that the EC shall contribute to the attainment of a high level of consumer protection) cannot justify the direct effect of a directive on consumer protection which has not been transposed into national law.

Indirect effect

Key Principle: **Where a directive is indirectly effective (i.e. not directly effective) national legislation must be interpreted in the light of the wording and purpose of the directive.**

Von Colson and Kamann v Land Nordhein-Westfalen (Case 14/83) 1984

Ms Von Colson and Ms Kamann had applied for posts as social workers in a German prison. The officials responsible for recruitment refused to appoint the two women, although they had been placed at the top of the list of applicants by the social work committee, because of the problems and risks associated with working in a male prison. They claimed that they should be granted a contract of employment or damages under Art.6 of Directive 76/207. The German courts made an Art.234 reference.

Held: (ECJ) (1) Art.6 of Directive 76/207 does not satisfy the requirements for creating direct effects. (2) The duty of Member States to achieve the results envisaged by the directive and their duty under Art.5 to ensure fulfilment of that obligation binds all authorities within the Member States including the courts. National courts must interpret and apply legislation adopted to implement a directive in the light of the wording and purpose of the directive in order to achieve the objective of the directive. [1986] E.C.R. 1891.

Commentary

(1) Rather than treating the question as one concerned with the supremacy of EC law over national law, the ECJ developed a rule of construction in *Von Colson* derived from Art.249 (ex 189) (Directive binding on Member State to whom addressed, with choice of form and method left to the national authorities) and Art.10 (ex 5) (Member States must take all appropriate measures to ensure fulfilment of the obligations arising from the Treaty or secondary legislation).

(2) In *Kolpinghuis Nijmegen* (Case 80/86) the ECJ repeated the formula in *Von Colson* but added that a directive cannot independently create criminal liability where its provisions are infringed. See also *Arcaro* (Case C-168/95) in which the ECJ held that, where a Member State has failed to transpose a directive, the obligation to interpret national law in line with EC law reaches a limit. An unimplemented directive may not, of itself, serve to determine or aggravate criminal liability of persons acting in contravention of the directive. For an application of the principle in the context of the First Companies Directive 68/15, see *Berlusconi* (Joined Cases C-387, 391 and 403/02).

(3) United Kingdom law provides for the implementation of indirectly effective EC law in s.2(2) of the ECA 1972.

Key Principle: **The obligation to interpret national law to comply with a directive applies regardless of whether the national law was adopted before or after the directive.**

Marleasing SA v La Commercial Internacional de Alimtacion SA (Case C-106/89) 1990
Marleasing SA had sued La Commercial and several other companies in the Spanish courts. M claimed that the defendant companies had been established by Barviesa, who owed M large sums of money, in order to put his assets beyond the reach of his creditors. M sought a declaration that the contract establishing the companies was void for lack of cause under the Spanish

Civil Code. La Commercial claimed that the action should be dismissed because lack of cause was not listed in Art.11 of Directive 68/151, which listed nullity grounds exhaustively. An Art.234 reference was made.

Held: (ECJ) In applying national law, whether the provisions in question were adopted before or after the directive, the national court must interpret it, as far as possible, in the light of the wording and purpose of the directive in order to achieve the result pursued by the directive and to comply with Art.249(3) (ex 189(3)). [1990] E.C.R. I-4135.

Commentary

(1) It followed from the ruling in *Marleasing* that the Spanish Civil Code had to be interpreted in line with the directive, thus excluding lack of cause as a ground for annulment of the contract.

(2) The obligation to interpret national law to conform with an EC obligation is stated to apply "as far as possible".

(3) In *Wagner Miret v Fondo de Garantia Salarial* (Case C-334/92) the ECJ accepted that it was impossible to interpret preexisting legislation so as to comply with Directive 80/987 on the protection of employees in the event of their employer's insolvency. In such circumstances the state may be obliged to compensate the applicant for his loss under the *Francovich* principle (see p.15).

Key Principle: **It is for the national courts to decide in each case whether it is possible to interpret national law to accord with a directive or whether it would distort the meaning of the national law.**

Webb v EMO Air Cargo (UK) Ltd 1992
Ms Webb was engaged by EMO for an indefinite term while another employee was on maternity leave. She was dismissed when she found that she, too, was pregnant. The House of Lords had to consider whether EMO was entitled to dismiss Ms Webb. This required the court to decide whether it could construe the Sex Discrimination Act 1975 in accord with the

Equal Treatment Directive 76/207. The House of Lords referred questions to the ECJ.

Held: (HL) It is for the United Kingdom court to construe domestic legislation in any field covered by an EC Directive so as to accord with the interpretation of the directive as laid down by the ECJ, if that can be done without distorting the meaning of the domestic legislation. [1993] 1 C.M.L.R. 259.

Commentary

(1) The ECJ ruled that it was a breach of Directive 76/207 to dismiss a female employee who was pregnant and who had been recruited for an unlimited term, even if she had been engaged as a maternity leave replacement (see Ch.14, p.186). The House of Lords applied the ruling and interpreted the United Kingdom law in accordance with the directive.

(2) *Webb v EMO* represents a clear statement by the House of Lords of the duty of the United Kingdom courts to give effect to EC law when interpreting national law. Webb was decided after *Marleasing* and should be contrasted with its earlier decision in *Duke v Reliance Systems* (HL, 1988) in which it had held that it would distort the meaning of the Sex Discrimination Act 1975 to interpret it so as to give effect to Directive 76/207.

(3) The ECJ upheld the liberal approach to statutory interpretation exemplified by cases such as *Marleasing* in two recent decisions. In *Centrosteel Srl v Adipol GmbH* (Case C-456/98) it held that the national court is bound, when applying provisions of domestic law, predating or postdating the relevant directive, to interpret those provisions, as far as possible, in the light of the wording and purpose of the directive, so that those provisions are applied in a manner consistent with the result pursued by the directive. In *Oceano Grupo Editorial SA v Quintero* and *Salvat Editores SA v Prades* (Joined Cases C-240/98 and C-244/98), it repeated this formula, adding (in the context of the Unfair Contract Terms Directive 93/113) that the requirement to interpret in conformity with the Directive requires the national court, in particular, to favour the interpretation which would allow it to decline of its own motion the jurisdiction conferred on it by an unfair term.

(4) The ECJ confirmed in *Maria Pupino* (Case C-105/03) that the duty to interpret national law in line with EC law applies in the area of Police and Judicial Co-operation. The EC had adopted a Framework Decision requiring Member States to guarantee victims the opportunity to be heard in criminal proceedings. Particularly vulnerable victims must benefit from specific treatment. This case arose in the context of criminal proceedings against a former nursery school teacher accused of various abusive practices against the children in her care, all of whom were under five years old at the time. The defendant opposed the Public Prosecutor's request for special arrangements to take the testimony of eight children who were witnesses and victims, arguing that it contravened Italian law. The national court made a reference to the ECJ under Art.234. (The ECJ has jurisdiction to give preliminary rulings on Framework Decisions where a Member State declares that it accepts this jurisdiction. Italy had made such a declaration.) The Court held that the national court must interpret national law as far as possible in conformity with the wording and purpose of the Framework decision, in order to attain the result which it envisages. The national court must be able to authorise young children claiming mistreatment to give their testimony in accordance with arrangements providing for a suitable level of protection.

Key Principle: **National provisions must not make it practically impossible or excessively difficult to exercise rights conferred by EC law.**

Metallgesellschaft Ltd, Hoechst Ag and Hoechst UK v Commissioners of Inland Revenue and H.M. Attorney General (Joined Cases C-379/98 & C-410/98) 2001
The applicants were subsidiaries whose parent companies were not resident within the same Member States (the UK and Germany). The subsidiaries challenged the resulting imposition of discriminatory corporation tax (ACT), seeking restitution or compensation in the form of interest which would otherwise have been due.

Held: (ECJ) (Old) Art.52 requires that resident subsidiaries and their non-resident parent should have an effective legal remedy in order to obtain reimbursement or reparation of the financial loss suffered and from which the Member State concerned has benefited as a result of the advance payment of corporation tax by the subsidiaries.

Commentary

(1) The ECJ did not accept the UK's argument that the applicant should have refused to comply with national tax law, seeking a remedy through directly effective EC law.

(2) An individual may not be prohibited from relying on Art.81 merely because he was a party to an anti-competitive agreement, unless he was significantly responsible for the breach.

State liability for breach of EC law

Key Principle: **A Member State will be liable for non-implementation of a directive in certain circumstances.**

Francovich, Bonifaci and others v Italy **(Cases C-6 & 9/90) 1991** Italy had failed to implement Directive 80/987 on the protection of workers in the event of insolvency. (The directive required the guarantee of payments of outstanding claims for remuneration and the creation of guarantee institutions to meet those claims.) Italy's breach was established by the ECJ in *Commission v Italy* (Case 22/87). Francovich and Bonifaci had outstanding claims against a company declared bankrupt in 1985. Unable to recover against the company they brought actions in the Italian courts against Italy, requesting that Italy should pay them compensation in the light of the obligation in the directive. Both national courts referred questions to the ECJ to determine the extent of a Member State's liability.

Held: (ECJ) Member States are obliged to compensate individuals for breaches of EC law for which they are responsible if three conditions are satisfied:

(1) The objective of the directive must include the conferring of rights for the benefit of individuals.

(2) The content of the rights must be identifiable from the directive.

(3) There must be a causal link between the breach and the damage. [1991] E.C.R. I-5357.

Commentary

(1) The ECJ in *Francovich* stated that the full effectiveness of EC law would be impaired if individuals were unable to obtain compensation when their rights were infringed by a breach attributable to a Member State. The principle of state liability is inherent in the scheme of the Treaty. The duty on Member States to compensate derives from Art.10 (ex 5) which obliges them to ensure fulfilment of their obligations under EC law.

(2) State liability under *Francovich* applies to obligations which may not be directly effective and provides a remedy in the event of non-implementation (or inadequate implementation) of EC law. Thus it prevents a state from relying on its own default in implementing EC law.

(3) The ruling has been of immense importance and has been extended and clarified in a number of later rulings.

(4) The High Court in *Three Rivers District Council v Governor and Company of the Bank of England* (1997) held that no action for state liability arose out of the First Banking Directive (the directive at issue in *Francovich*) as the directive did not intend to confer rights on individuals. This decision is hard to reconcile with that of the Italian court in *Francovich*; where the court found that the directive did confer rights on the individual members of a group, but that F himself was outside the group.

Key Principle: **States are liable for breaches of EC law where the breach is sufficiently serious.**

Brasserie du Pêcheur SA v Germany (Case C-46/93) and R. v Secretary of State for Transport Ex p. Factortame Ltd (No.3) (Joined Cases C-46/93 and C-48/93) 1996
These cases both concerned the question of the extent of state liability where legislation had been adopted in contravention of directly effective rights. *Brasserie du Pêcheur* arose out of a claim by a French brewery against Germany for losses incurred as a result of the German Beer Purity laws which had been found by the ECJ to infringe Art.28 (ex 30) (Case 178/84). *Factortame* (see p.5) had led to a finding that the Merchant Shipping Act 1988

infringed EC law. The Spanish trawler owners claimed compensation from the United Kingdom courts. An Art.234 reference was made to the ECJ.

Held: (ECJ) Where a Member State acts in a field where it has a wide discretion, it will be liable to an individual for breach of EC law provided:

(1) the rule of law infringed is intended to confer rights on individuals;

(2) the breach is sufficiently serious;

(3) there is a direct causal link between the breach and the damage. [1996] 1 C.M.L.R. 889.

Commentary

(1) The first and third conditions correspond to *Francovich*. However, the position of the Member States was compared with that of the EC institutions under Art.288 (ex 215) (see Ch.6, p.67). The EC institutions are liable in relation to legislative measures involving choices of economic policy where the breach is "sufficiently serious", i.e. when it is "manifest and grave" under the *Schoppenstedt* formula: see Ch.6, pp.67–68.

(2) It was held that reparation may not be made conditional onfault or on a prior finding by the ECJ and that the amount must be commensurate with the damage sustained. No temporal restriction was placed on the effect of the judgment.

(3) The German Federal Court applied the ruling of the ECJ in *Brasserie du Pêcheur v Germany* in 1996. It held that there was no direct causal link between the breach of Art.28 (ex 30) and the applicant's loss. It also found that the infringement in relation to additives was not sufficiently serious. The brewer's claim against the German Government thus failed.

(4) The United Kingdom Divisional Court in *Factortame* (No.5) held in 1997 that the trawler owners were entitled to damages, but not to punitive damages. The House of Lords upheld the earlier findings of fault by the British Government, namely that there had been a sufficiently serious

breach, leaving unchanged the earlier ruling on damages: *R. v Secretary of State for Transport Ex p. Factortame* (Decision of October 28, 1999) HL.

Key Principle: **Incorrect implementation of an imprecisely worded directive does not necessarily give rise to state liability.**

R. v H.M. Treasury Ex p. British Telecommunications Plc (Case C-392/93) 1996
BT claimed that the United Kingdom had incorrectly implemented Directive 90/531 covering the procurement (purchasing) procedures of bodies contracting in the telecommunications sector (e.g. BT and Mercury). In particular, BT alleged that the procedures adopted by the United Kingdom for exemption had put BT at a competitive disadvantage. The United Kingdom court referred questions to the ECJ.

Held: (ECJ) The three conditions in *Brasserie du Pêcheur/ Factortame* must be satisfied. However, when transposing the directive into national law, the United Kingdom Government had not gravely and manifestly disregarded the limits on the exercise of their power. The breach was not sufficiently serious to impose liability. [1996] All E.R. (EC) 411.

Commentary

(1) The ECJ appears in *Ex p. British Telecommunications* to have accepted that the breach was not sufficiently serious because the obligation in the directive was imprecisely worded and could reasonably have borne the interpretation placed on it by the United Kingdom Government. No guidance had been provided to the United Kingdom by the ECJ and the Commission had not objected to the United Kingdom's implementing regulations.

(2) See also *Denkavit International v Bundesamt für Ernahring* (Case C-283, 291 & 292/94) which also involved incorrect transposition of a directive. The ECJ finding that the breach was not sufficiently serious to lead to liability on the part of

Germany was influenced by the fact that most other Member States had adopted a similar approach to Germany's.

Key Principle: **The mere fact of infringement of EC law may be enough to establish the existence of a sufficiently serious breach.**

R. v Minister of Agriculture, Fisheries and Food Ex p. Hedley Lomas (Ireland) Ltd (Case C-5/94) 1996

MAFF refused to grant licences to enable Hedley Lomas to export live sheep to Spain because it considered that Spain had not implemented properly an EC directive dealing with the preslaughter condition of certain animals. The Commission investigated but found no breach by Spain. It informed the United Kingdom that its export ban infringed Art.29 (ex 34) and was not justified under Art.30 (ex 36). When proceedings were brought in the United Kingdom courts, an Art.234 reference was made.

Held: (ECJ) (1) Recourse to Art.30 (ex 36) is impossible where harmonisation has occurred.

(2) A Member State may not act unilaterally to avoid a breach of EC law by another Member State.

(3) Where a Member State does not have to make legislative choices or has only reduced discretion, the mere fact of infringement of EC law may be enough to establish a sufficiently serious breach.

(4) It is for the national court to determine whether there is a causal link between duty and the damage.

(5) If state liability is established, the state must make good any loss in accordance with its domestic law on liability. [1996] All E.R. (EC) 493.

Commentary

(1) See also *Dillenkofer v Federal Republic of Germany* (Joined Cases C-178, etc./94): intentional fault is not an essential precondition to state liability. Here, the German Government had failed to implement the Package Holidays Dir-

ective by the deadline. The ECJ held that failure to implement a directive on time was a sufficiently serious breach.

(2) In *Rechberger v Austria* (Case C-140/97), in another case
involving the Package Holidays Directive, the ECJ found
that incorrect transposition of the directive, preventing
reimbursement of money in the event of the insolvency of
the travel organiser was a sufficiently serious breach. Austria
had no margin of discretion over the implementation of the
directive.

(3) In *Konle v Austria* (Case C-302/97) the ECJ sought to clarify
the position on state liability for breach of EC law by states
with a federal structure (like Austria). The ECJ held that it is
for each Member State to ensure that individuals obtain
compensation for damage caused to them by breach of EC
law, whichever public authority is responsible for the breach
and for payment of compensation. There is no need under
EC law to change the law relating to the distribution of
power and responsibility within public bodies, provided it is
no more difficult for an individual to bring an action for
state liability for breach of EC law than to bring an action in
relation to rights deriving under national law.

(4) The ECJ provided further guidance as to discretion in
relation to what is a sufficiently serious breach in *Haim v
Kassenzahrnäarzliche Vereinigung Nordhein* (Case 424/97). It
held that the existence and scope of discretion must be
determined by EC and not national law. It follows that
discretion conferred on an individual by national law is
irrelevant. EC law does not preclude a public law body, in
addition to the Member State, from being liable to make
reparation for loss and damage caused to individuals as a
result of measures which it took in breach of EC law.

(5) It was clear from the decision in *Brasserie du Pêcheur* that
losses arising from judicial decisions may, in principle, give
rise to state liability. In *Köbler v Austria* (Case C-224/01) the
ECJ held that state liability can arise from an infringement
of EC law by a decision of a national court of last resort
only exceptionally where the court has manifestly infringed
the law. The case arose out of a claim by an Austrian
professor for recognition of time spent working in universities in other EU Member States for the purpose of a long
service increment. (Austrian law required ten years as a
professor at an Austrian university to qualify.) The national

court withdrew a request for a preliminary ruling from the ECJ. As a result, the applicant lost the increment. The applicant sued the Austrian government for infringement of state liability. This time a preliminary reference was made to the ECJ. The Court held that various factors should be considered when deciding whether the breach was manifest, namely the degree of clarity and precision of the rule infringed, whether the breach was intentional, whether or not the error of law was excusable, the position taken by a Community institution, and non-compliance by the court in its obligation to make a referral to the ECJ under Art.234(3).

2. THE INSTITUTIONS OF THE EC AND EU

The European Parliament

Key Principle: **Failure to consult the EP, where required by the Treaty, is a breach of an essential procedural requirement.**

Roquette Frères S.A. v Council (Case 138/79) 1980

The Council adopted a regulation before it had received the opinion of the EP under Art.34(3) (ex 40(3)). It was challenged by a producer affected by the measure. (See Ch.5, p.59).

Held: (ECJ) Consultation under Art.34(3) is the means whereby the EP participates in the legislative process of the EC. Failure to consult was a breach of an essential procedural requirement, as a result of which the measure concerned was void. [1980] E.C.R. 3393.

Commentary
The ECJ stated in *Roquette Frères* that consultation "reflects at Community level the fundamental democratic principle that the peoples should take part in the exercise of power through the intermediary of an intermediate assembly".

Key Principle: **The EP may take action in the ECJ to protect its prerogative.**

EP v Council (Re Students' Rights) (Case C-295/90)

The Commission proposed a directive on residence rights for students undertaking vocational courses based on Art.7(2)(now repealed) of the Treaty. This basis would have involved the use of the co-operation procedure, with qualified majority voting. After the EP's opinion had been received the draft was submitted to the Council which amended the legal basis to Art.308 (ex 235), the general power for which a unanimous vote was required.

Held: (ECJ) The EP may bring actions to safeguard its prerogatives. [1992] 3 C.M.L.R. 281.

Commentary

Although the EP was not at that time expressly covered by (old) Art.173, the fact that the Council's action deprived the EP of a second reading was enough to justify a challenge. This right, where there is a threat to the prerogative of the EP, was expressly provided in the revised wording of Art.173 (now 230) following amendment by the Maastricht Treaty. (See Ch.5, p.53.)

Key Principle: **If the Council or Commission fails to act, in infringement of the Treaty, the EP may bring an action in the ECJ: Art.232 (ex 175).**

EP v Council (Case 13/83) 1985

The EP sought a declaration that the Council had infringed the EEC Treaty by failing to adopt a Common Transport Policy. The Council objected, claiming that the EP lacked competence to bring an action under Art.232 (ex 175).

Held: (ECJ) The EP had capacity to bring an action under Art.232 and had observed the conditions of that provision in bringing the action. The action was upheld in part, but rejected where the obligation was too vague to be enforceable. (See Ch. 5, p.62).

The Council of the European Union

Key Principle: **Regulations, directives and decisions adopted jointly by the EP and the Council, and such acts adopted by the Council or Commission, shall state the reasons on which they are based and shall refer to any proposals or opinions which were required to be obtained under the Treaty: Art.253 (ex 190).**

Key Principle: **If action by the EC is necessary, in the course of the operation of the common market, to attain one of the objectives of the EC and the Treaty has not provided the necessary powers, the Council shall take the appropriate measures acting on a proposal from the Commission and after consulting the EP.**

Commission v Council (Case 45/86) 1987

The Commission brought annulment proceedings under Art.230 (ex 173) (see Ch.5) against two regulations adopted by the Council relating to generalised tariff preferences for products from developing countries. The Commission claimed that there was no explicit legal basis stated in the measures. The Council argued that it had intended to base the measures on both Arts 133 (ex 113) (the Common Commercial Policy) and 308 (ex 235).

Held: (ECJ) It follows from the wording of Art.308 (ex 235) that its use as the legal basis for a measure is justified only where no other provision of the Treaty gives the EC institutions the necessary power to adopt the measure in question. As Art.133 (ex 113) would have provided an appropriate legal basis, the Council was not justified in relying on Art.308 (ex 235). [1987] E.C.R. 1493.

Commentary

(1) The choice of legal basis determines the procedure which is followed in the adoption of the measure. Article 308 (ex 235), unlike Art.133 (ex 113), requires unanimity in the Council, thus making it possible for individual states to veto a proposed measure.

(2) As a result of the Maastricht Treaty amendments, the Council has become known as the Council of the EU, with responsibility extending beyond the area of legal control under the EC Treaty to the areas of political co-operation (the Common Foreign and Security Policy, and Police and Judicial Co-operation, as the third pillar was renamed by the ToA). The other institutions remain institutions of the EC.

Key Principle: **The choice of legal base must be based on objective factors which are amenable to judicial review.**

Commission v Council (Case C-300/89) 1991

The Commission brought annulment proceedings under Art.230 (ex 173) against the Council in relation to a directive harmonising programmes to eliminate pollution caused by waste from the titanium dioxide industry. The directive in question had been based on Art.130s (now 175) which (following the consultation procedure under the EC Treaty prior to amendment by the TEU) enabled the Council to adopt measures relating to environment protection by unanimity, on a proposal from the Commission after consulting the EP and the Economic and Social Committee. The Commission claimed that the measure should have been adopted under Art.95 (ex 100a) (the co-operation procedure, requiring qualified majority voting and two consultations with the EP) as a single market measure.

Held: (ECJ) The measure should have been based on Art.95 (ex 100a), not Art.175 (ex 130s). [1991] E.C.R. I-2867.

Commentary

(1) While the directive displayed features relating both to the environment and to the establishment and functioning of the internal market, recourse to a dual basis was excluded by the ECJ. An EC measure cannot be treated as an environmental measure merely because it pursues objectives of environmental protection. Action to harmonise national rules on industrial production with a view to eliminating distortion of competition is covered by Art.95 (ex 100a).

(2) This case was considered under the Treaty of Rome prior to amendment by the Maastricht Treaty. After amendment by the TEU, the co-decision procedure providing for more extensive consultation with the EP, in Art.251 (ex 189b) governed the adoption of internal market rules. Under co-decision the EP became jointly responsible for the adoption of legislation. Environmental measures under Art.175 (ex 130s) are, after amendment by the ToA, also adopted under co-decision, instead of the consultation procedure.

(3) In *EP v Council* (Case C-42/97) the EP, by contrast, sought to argue that a Council decision on the adoption of a programme to promote linguistic diversity in the EC should have a dual legal base. The ECJ concluded that the effects on culture were only indirectly incidental; the measure was essentially economic. As a result, it was appropriate for the measure to have been based on Art.130 EC (now, after amendment, Art.157 EC) on industry rather than Art.128 (now, after amendment, Art.151 EC (culture)).

(4) The EP mounted another challenge to a measure adopted by the Council in *EP v Council* (Joined Cases C-164 & 165/97). The regulations in question had been adopted

under Art.37 EC (then 37 EC). They were intended to protect forests in the EC from atmospheric pollution and fire. This time the ECJ held that the measures were primarily environmental, even though there would have been repercussions for agriculture, and allowed the EP's application. See also *EP v Council* (Case C-189/97) in which the EP failed in its challenge over the adoption of the budget under Art.300(3) (ex 228(3)) EC. The EP claimed that the measure was an agreement with important budgetary implications requiring the EP's assent, a claim ultimately rejected by the ECJ.

(5) *Netherlands v EP* and *Council* (Case C-377/98) arose out of a challenge by the Netherlands (a long-standing opponent of genetic manipulation of animals and plants) to Directive 98/44 on the legal protection of biotechnical inventions. The Directive lists which inventions involving plants, animals or the human body may be patented. Member States are required to allow the patenting of inventions with an industrial application, making it possible to use biological material. The Dutch government sought to annul the Directive, claiming that it should not be possible to patent plant, animal or human material. It was supported in the action by Italy and Norway. A number of grounds were used including the use of wrong legal base (old Art.100a). The ECJ dismissed all the claims, holding that the measure was an internal market measure and so properly adopted under (old) Art.100a, compliance with subsidiary was implicit in the recitals to the Directive: there was no uncertainty, no breach of international law, no infringement of rights of human dignity and no breach of procedural rules.

(6) In *R. v Secretary of State for Health Ex p. British American Tobacco (Investments) Ltd* (Case C-491/01) the legal base of a directive was again at issue, this time in relation to tobacco advertising. The case arose under an Art.234 reference from proceedings before the High Court in which judicial review was sought in relation to the intention and/ or obligation of the UK government to transpose the Directive into UK law. Directive 90/239 was adopted under (old) Arts 95 and 133 of the Treaty, recasting an earlier directive, providing a stronger health warning. The national court sought to clarify whether the Directive was invalid, by lacking an appropriate legal base. The ECJ found that where an EC act has a twofold purpose and one of these is predominant, the

act must be founded on that as the predominant one. Where, exceptionally, the act pursues several objectives which are indissolubly linked, it may have several legal bases. In the case in question, Art.95 was found to be the correct legal base. The incorrect reference to Art.133 did not, however, make the Directive invalid. It was no more than a formal defect. Having found, in addition, that there were no breaches of the principles of subsidiarity and proportionality (amongst other matters), the ECJ ruled that the Directive was valid.

Key Principle: **Where the Treaty confers a specific task on the Commission, it also confers on it the powers which are indispensable to carry out the task.**

Key Principle: **The Commission shall have the task of promoting close co-operation between Member States in the social field. To this end the Commission shall act in close contact with Member States by making studies, delivering opinions and arranging consultations both on problems arising at national level and on those of concern to international organisations: Art.137 (ex 118).**

Germany, France, Netherlands, Denmark and the United Kingdom v Commission (Joined Cases 281, 283 and 287/85) 1987
Germany and the other applicant states sought annulment under Art.230 (ex 173) of Decision 85/381 in relation to the migration policy of non-member countries. The challenge was brought on the grounds that such a policy was outside the social field and that the arrangement of consultation under Art.137 (ex 118) did not empower the Commission to adopt binding measures.

Held: (ECJ) (1) The promotion of the integration into the workforce of non-member countries must be held to be within the social field within the meaning of Art.137 (ex 118), in so far as it is linked to employment.

(2) The promotion of cultural integration goes beyond the social field but may be justified under Art.137(2) (ex 118(2)) (power to arrange consultations). [1987] E.C.R. 3203.

Commentary
The ECJ exercised care in this judgement to make it clear that the Commission's power to take binding decisions (not explicitly provided in Art.137 (ex 118(2)) is limited to procedural matters.

Key Principle: **Citizens of the EU and natural or legal persons residing or having a registered office in one of the Member States shall have a right of access to EP, Council or Commission documents: Art.255(1) EC (following amendment by the ToA).**

Key Principle: **The public shall have access to measures adopted by the Council unless the release of such documents would undermine the protection of the public interest, individual privacy, commercial and industrial secrecy, the EC's financial interests or confidentiality requested by natural or legal persons: Art.1 of Decision 93/731.**

Carvel & Guardian Newspapers v Council (Case T(194/94) 1995
Carvel, the European Affairs Editor of the Guardian, requested various documents relating to meetings of the Social Affairs and Justice Council in 1993 and the Agriculture Committee in 1994. The Council's Secretariat refused, stating that the documents related directly to the deliberations of the Council and could not be disclosed. The applicants challenged the decision under Art.230 (ex 173).

Held: (CFI) Decision 93/731 requires the balancing of the applicants' interests in gaining access with the Council's interests in maintaining confidentiality. By automatically refusing access to the documents the Council had failed to exercise discretion in accordance with the decision. [1995] 3 C.M.L.R. 359.

Commentary

   (1) After the ruling of the CFI the Council agreed to facilitate the release of minutes of meetings, to broadcast debates on matters of public interest and to release details of votes on

legislative acts. Carvel remains dissatisfied and is pursuing a further action against the Council.

(2) The ToA consolidated various changes on transparency of documents which had been introduced in the Council Rules of Procedure, the code of conduct on access to documents and consequential Council and Commission decisions. The principle in Art.255(1) EC is subject to the Council's power in Art.255(2) to determine the "general principles and limits on grounds of public and private interest governing the right of access to documents" within two years of the ToA coming into force.

(3) In *Svenska Journalistforbundet v Council* (Case T(174/95) the CFI interpreted Art.1 of the Regulation as meaning that the Council must consider in relation to each document requested whether disclosure would undermine one of the matters referred to in para.1 of the Code of Conduct concerning Public Access to Council and Commission Documents (including public interest, protection of the individual and privacy, etc.). Similar considerations govern the release of Commission documents: *Interporc v Commission* (Case T-124/96).

(4) In *Council v Hautala* (Case C-353/99P) the Council appealed against a decision of the CFI which had annulled its decision to refuse Ms Hautala, an MEP, access to a report on conventional arms policy. The refusal was based on Decision 93/731 regarding public access to documents, under which the Council may refuse access to a document in order to protect public interest in the field of international relations. The Council stated that the report contained sensitive information which would harm the EU's relations with non-Member States. The ECJ emphasised that the public should have the widest possible access to Council and Commission documents. If a document contains confidential information, partial access must be considered. Refusal of partial access was a disproportionate measure. The Council may not systematically limit the public's right of access to documents.

3. FUNDAMENTAL RIGHTS AND GENERAL PRINCIPLES

Key Principle: **Fundamental rights and the general principles of EC law are protected by the ECJ.**

Stauder v City of Ulm (Case 29/69) 1969

A Commission regulation provided for the recipients of welfare benefits to receive free butter. When the scheme was implemented, the German Government required beneficiaries to produce a coupon bearing their name and address. Stauder claimed that the German decision implementing the scheme infringed the general principles of EC law. An Art.234 (ex 177) reference was made to the ECJ by the German administrative court.

Held: (ECJ) The provision in issue contained nothing capable of prejudicing the fundamental human rights enshrined in the general principles of EC law and protected by the Court [1969] E.C.R. 419.

Commentary

(1) The tentative statement in *Stauder* is the first acknowledgment by the ECJ that fundamental rights are recognised by EC law. In its subsequent case law the ECJ has developed its approach to fundamental rights, providing a mechanism to review that validity of action by the EC institutions and by the Member States. Fundamental rights and general principles are most often invoked in annulment proceedings under Art.230 (ex 173) (see Ch.5), to claim damages under Art.288 (ex 215) (see Ch.6) and as a guide to the interpretation of EC law (see Ch.1).

(2) General principles derive from: (a) international law, e.g. the European Convention of Human Rights, (b) principles which are accepted by the domestic legal systems of the Member States and (c) the decisions of the ECJ.

(3) The Charter of Fundamental Rights was proclaimed at the Nice European Summit in December 1999. It was based on existing law from various sources particularly the European Convention on Human Rights and Fundamental Freedoms (ECHR). The Charter is divided into seven chapters headed Dignity (including freedom from torture and slavery), Free-

doms (liberty, association, expression, property, private and family life), Equality (similar to Art.13 of the EC Treaty, with further references to rights of children, the elderly and persons with disabilities), Solidarity (labour rights based on the earlier European Social Charter), Citizens' rights (EU citizenship, right to good administration access to documents), Justice (e.g. right to a fair trial), and finally, General Clauses on the scope of Charter. It should be noted that if the Constitutional Treaty is ratified, the Charter will be incorporated into the body of the Treaty.

Key Principle: **Respect for fundamental rights forms an integral part of the general principles of law protected by the ECJ.**

Internationale Handelsgesellschaft mbH v Einfuhr-und Vorratsstelle für Getreide und Futtermittel (Case 11/70) 1970
The applicants had obtained a licence to export maize from Germany, conditional under an EC regulation on lodging a deposit which acted as a guarantee that the exportation would be carried out while the licence was valid. As the exportation was not completed during the validity of the licence, the German administrative authorities ordered the forfeiture of a large part of the deposit. The applicants challenged the forfeiture on the basis that it contravened certain principles of German law in the Frankfurt administrative court, which made an Art.234 reference to the ECJ.

Held: (ECJ) The validity of a measure of EC law cannot be affected by allegations that it contravenes national fundamental rights or national constitutional principles.
(2) The protection of fundamental rights, while inspired by the constitutional traditions common to the Member States, must be ensured within the framework and structure of the objectives of the EC [1970] E.C.R. 1125.

Commentary

(1) See also *Nold v Commission* (Case 4/73) in which the ECJ declared that it would not uphold measures which are incompatible with fundamental rights recognised and protected by the constitutions of the Member States.

(2) In the early years the German Constitutional Court did notaccept the supremacy of EC law on fundamental rights expressed in decisions such as Handelsgesellschaft. This view was modified in *Wünsche Handelsgesellschaft* (1987) where the German court accepted that the protection of fundamental rights under EC law had reached the level of German law. However, in *Brunner v EU Treaty* (1994) the Constitutional Court reasserted its right to review the legitimacy of EC law (see Ch.1).

(3) In *Connolly v Commission* (Case C-274/99P), Bernard Connolly, then a high ranking official in the Commission, for personal reasons, published a book in 1995 entitled *The Rotten Heart of Europe*, which was highly critical of the Commission. After being removed from his post in 1996 he sought unsuccessfully to annul the decision ordering the removal before the CFI. He then appealed to the ECJ which upheld the decision of the CFI. The ECJ reaffirmed its support for fundamental rights including freedom of expression under the ECHR, but held that the protection of the rights of the institutions, responsible for carrying out tasks in the public interest, justifies the restriction. The ECJ was required to strike a fair balance between the individual's fundamental right to freedom of expression and the legitimate concern of the institutions to ensure that their officials and employees fulfil their duties.

Legal certainty

Non-retroactivity

Key Principle: **Penal provisions may not take effect retroactively.**

R. v Kirk (Case 63/83) 1984

Captain Kirk, a Danish fisherman, was charged with fishing in the United Kingdom's 12 mile coastal fishing zone, contrary to United Kingdom law. Although the United Kingdom was entitled under the Act of Accession to exclude non-United Kingdom fishing vessels from the 12 mile zone until December 31, 1982, Captain Kirk had been fishing on January 6, 1983. The EC subsequently adopted a regulation permitting the United Kingdom to maintain the exclusion for a further 10 years, backdated to January 1, 1983. The United Kingdom court made an Art.234 (ex 177) reference. [1984] E.C.R. 2689.

Held: (ECJ) Non-retroactivity of penal provisions is common to all the Member States and enshrined in Art.7 of the ECHR. It is one of the general principles of EC law.

Commentary

(1) The duty to interpret national law in accordance with EC law reaches its limits in the context of the general principles of law, particularly the principle of non-retroactivity. In *X* (Case C-60/02), the Austrian court sought clarification of the legality of imposing penalties for breach of EC law. This action arose out of a request by Rolex for a judicial investigation into persons unknown, following the discovery of a consignment of counterfeit watches in transit between Italy and Poland. Austrian law only permitted a judicial review where the conduct involved a criminal offence. The importation and exportation of counterfeit goods was an offence. Mere transit was not an offence under Austrian law, although it was an offence under an EC Regulation. The ECJ held that, if the national court considered that mere transit was not an office, the principle of non-retroactivity of penalties would prohibit the imposition of criminal penalties for such conduct, even though the national law was contrary to EC law.

(2) The ECJ has upheld a number of individual provisions of the ECHR as general principles of EC law: see e.g. *National Panasonic (UK) Ltd v Commission* (Case 136/79): Art.8 (right to privacy); VBVB v Commission (Cases 43 & 63/82): Art.10 (right to expression).

(3) While the EC is not a party to the ECHR it has recognised the importance of fundamental rights in Art.6(1) (ex F(1) TEU), stating that the Union is founded on the principles of liberty, democracy, respect for human rights and fundamental freedoms and the rule of law, principles which are common to the Member States. Article 6(2) (ex F(2) of the TEU) provides that the Union shall respect fundamental rights, as guaranteed by the ECHR and as they result from the constitutional traditions common to the Member States, as general principles of EC law. Article 7 (ex F(1) of the TEU) is a new provision introduced by the ToA. It empowers the Council to determine that a Member State has committed a persistent and serious breach of human rights, in which case it may decide to suspend the voting rights of the offending state.

(4) The EC itself has fallen foul of the ECHR. In *Matthews* (ECHR), the applicant, a resident of Gibraltar, brought a claim before the European Court of Human Rights following her exclusion from voting in the EP. The Court of Human rights ruled in 1999 that the limited status for Gibraltar residents provided by the Direct Elections Act 1976 infringed Art.3 of Protocol 1 of the ECHR (right to free elections). As the Act was in fact a Treaty, the ECJ did not have the capacity to review it, thus depriving the applicant of a remedy if she had not pursued her claim before the Court of Human rights.

Legitimate expectations

Key Principle: **EC measures must not infringe the legitimate expectations of those concerned in the absence of overriding public interest.**

Mulder v Minister van Landbouw en Visserig (Case 120/86) 1988
Mulder and other milk producers decided not to deliver milk for five years under an EC scheme to reduce an excess supply of milk. After that time they were unable to resume deliveries because provision under an EC regulation was based on a reference year during the five years of non-delivery.

Held: (ECJ) Where a producer has been encouraged by an EC provision to suspend marketing in the general interest and against the payment of a premium he may legitimately expect not to be subjected to restrictions because he has acted on the provision. [1988] E.C.R. 2321.

Commentary
An expectation is only legitimate where it is reasonable rather than speculative. Challenges to EC legislation based on a breach of legitimate expectations rarely succeed.

Proportionality

Key Principle: **Measures should not exceed what is appropriate and necessary to achieve the objectives in question.**

R. v Intervention Board for Agricultural Produce, Ex p. Man(Sugar) (Case 181/84) 1986
As a result of applying for an export licence four hours late the Commission ruled that the entire deposit was forfeit under the

terms of a regulation. The Divisional Court in the United Kingdom made an Art.234 reference.

Held: (ECJ) The forfeiture of the entire deposit was a disproportionate penalty for a minor breach. The regulation was annulled to the extent that it required the forfeiture. [1985] E.C.R. 2889.

Commentary

(1) Proportionality, like a number of other general principles, derives from German law, although there are some similarities with reasonableness in English law. Proportionality operates by weighing the objectives of legislation against the means by which they are achieved. The principle operates to restrain public authorities from imposing unnecessarily restrictive measures.

(2) Proportionality is frequently invoked in the context of single market measures. Under the *Cassis de Dijon* principle (see Ch.8, p.79) restrictions on imports may be permissible if necessary to justify a mandatory requirement provided they are not disproportionate. (In *Cassis* (Case-120/78) it was disproportionate to ban the sale of drinks below a certain alcohol level. Labelling would have provided the customer with sufficient information.) Proportionality is incorporated in the principle of subsidiarity under Art.5 (ex 3b) (see p.39 below).

Equality

Key Principle: **Persons in similar situations should be treated alike unless differential treatment is objectively justified.**

Sabbatini v EP (Case 20/71) 1972
Mrs Sabbatini sought the annulment of decisions whereby the expatriation allowance she had previously received from the EP was withdrawn following her marriage. The allowance was payable to the "head of the family", normally considered to be the husband except in cases of serious illness or invalidity.

Held: (ECJ) Determination of the status of expatriate must be dependent on uniform criteria, irrespective of sex. The decisions taken with regard to the applicant were annulled. [1972] E.C.R. 345.

Commentary

(1) The EC Treaty recognises the principle of equality (or non-discrimination) on grounds of nationality (Art.12 (ex 6) EC, sex (Art.141 (ex 119): equal pay for equal work) and against producers or consumers under the CAP (Art.34(3) (ex 40(3)). Equality of treatment has been extended by secondary legislation into such areas as access to employment and housing (Directive 76/207). Equality of treatment is essential to secure the free movement of goods, persons, services and capital (e.g. Art.30 (ex 36): exception to the free movement of goods, provided there is no discrimination on grounds of nationality. See Ch.8.). The ECJ has applied the principle imaginatively to meet the demands of the single market. See e.g. *Cowan v Tresor Public* (Case 186/87): Ch.11, p.135.

(2) For two recent examples of a breach of the principle of equality by the Italian government, see *Commission v Italy* (Case C-224/00) and *Commission v Italy* (Case C-388/01). In Case C-224/00 Italy was found to have infringed Art.12 (ex 6) of the Treaty by maintaining in force a provision of the Italian Highway Code for different and disproportionate treatment of offenders according to the place of registration of their vehicle, effectively discriminating against nationals of other Member States not resident in Italy. In Case C-388/01 Italy was found to have infringed both Arts 12 and 49 (see Ch.11) by applying differential rates for admission charges to museums, monuments, art galleries etc. The rates favoured Italian nationals and persons resident in Italy aged 60, 65 or above, but excluded tourists and non-residents.

Key Principle: **The Equal Treatment Directive should be interpreted liberally and should not be limited in scope to discrimination on grounds of gender.**

P v S (Case C-13/94) 1996
P was employed as a manager by Cornwall County Council. He was taken on to work as a male employee, but informed his employers that he intended to undergo treatment for gender reassignment. After taking sick leave, P was not permitted to

return to work in a female gender role. The final surgical operation took place after the expiry of notice of dismissal. P claimed for unfair dismissal before an industrial tribunal, claiming discrimination on grounds of sex. The tribunal made a request for an Art.234 ruling to the ECJ to clarify the meaning of the Equal Treatment Directive in relation to transsexuals.

Held: (ECJ) Art.5(1) of the Equal Treatment Directive 76/207 precludes the dismissal of a transsexual for a reason arising from the gender reassignment of the person concerned [1996] ECR I-2143.

Commentary

(1) Art.5(1) of Directive 76/207 provided that application of the principle with regard to working conditions including the conditions governing dismissal means that men and women shall be guaranteed the same conditions without discrimination on grounds of sex. Article 5 was deleted by Directive 2002/73, amending Directive 76/207.

(2) The ECJ in *P v S* followed the submissions of Advocate-General Tesauro that transsexuals do not constitute a third sex and were therefore protected by the Directive against discrimination on the grounds of sex, he submitted that respect for fundamental rights is one of the general principles of EC law, and that the elimination of discrimination on grounds of sex forms part of those fundamental rights. The ECJ stated that dismissal of a person due to an intention to carry out treatment for gender reassignment is contrary to Directive 76/207.

(3) For an example of the application in the UK by the Employment Appeals Tribunal of the approach adopted in *P v S*, see *Chessington World of Adventures Ltd v Reed* (1997) (dismissal following gender reassignment surgery from male to female).

(4) For a more conservative approach after *P v S*, see *Grant v South West Trains* (Case C-249/96), in which the ECJ held that Directive 76/207 does not cover issues of sexual orientation. (The facts of this case concerned a claim in the UK for the special travel concessions to cover same sex partners.) A different result may be achieved in such circumstances in the future, following amendment to the Treaty by the ToA.

Article 13 (ex 6a) EC empowers the Council to take appropriate action to combat discrimination based on sex, racial or ethnic origin, religion or belief, disability, age or sexual orientation. Two directives based on Art.13 were adopted in 2000, Directive 2000/43 on equal treatment between persons irrespective of racial or ethnic origin, and Directive 2000/78 providing a general framework for equal treatment in employment and occupation. See Ch.14, pp.193–194

Procedural rights

Right to a hearing

Key Principle: **A person whose interests are affected by a decision must be given the opportunity to be heard.**

Transocean Marine Paints Association v Commission (Case 17/74) 1974
The Commission reached a competition decision concerning exemption under Art.85(3) of an agreement between the undertakings making up the Association without hearing the Association's observations. The Association challenged the decision under Art.230 (ex 173).

Held: (ECJ) Interested parties have a right to be heard. The offending part of the decision was annulled (see Ch.5, p.53). [1974] E.C.R. 1063.

Commentary
The principle of the right to a hearing was confirmed in the case of *Ismeri Europa Srl v Court of Auditors* (Case C-315/99P) in which the ECJ dismissed an appeal against a decision of the CFI arising from an application for damages allegedly suffered by the applicant as a result of criticisms made by the Court of Auditors in its report in 1996. The ECJ held that there was no breach of the principle by the Court of Auditors as it was not bound to submit drafts of its reports to third parties such as the applicant.

Right to effective judicial control

Key Principle: **The individual is entitled to effective judicial control.**

Johnston v Chief Constable of the Royal Ulster Constabulary (Case 222/84) 1986
Mrs Johnston, a member of the full-time Reserve of the Royal

Ulster Constabulary (RUC), brought an action before an industrial tribunal challenging the decision of the Chief Constable of the RUC not to renew her contract and to refuse her training in firearms. The Chief Constable had decided, in the light of the large number of police officers killed in Northern Ireland, that male police officers would carry firearms in future. Women would not be equipped with firearms and would not receive firearms training. In the industrial tribunal the Chief Constable produced a certificate issued by the Secretary of State for Northern Ireland, stating that Mrs Johnston's contract had not been renewed in order to safeguard national security and to protect public safety and public order. Under Art.53 of the Northern Ireland Order the certificate was considered to be "conclusive evidence of purpose". Mrs Johnston claimed that the action contravened Art.6 of Directive 76/207 (obligation on Member States to introduce measures to enable applicants to pursue equal treatment claims before the courts). (See Ch.14, p.190).

Held: (ECJ) The principle of judicial control in Art.6 of Directive 76/207 reflects Arts 6 and 13 of the ECHR. It entitles all persons to an effective remedy in a competent court against measures which they consider contrary to the principle of equal treatment for men and women. The national courts must interpret a provision such as Art.53 of the Northern Ireland Order in the light of Directive 76/207.

Commentary
Other procedural rights that have been recognised by the ECJ include the duty to give reasons: *UNECTEF v Heylens* (Case 222/86); and the right to protection against self-incrimination: *Orkem v Commission* (Case 374/87) and *Solvay v Commission* (Case 27/88) (in the context of criminal proceedings only, and therefore not applicable to the competition investigations in question).

Subsidiarity

Key Principle: **The EC must act within the limits of the powers conferred on it by the Treaty. In areas outside the EC's exclusive competence, the EC must act in accordance with the principle of subsidiarity only if the proposed action cannot be sufficiently achieved by the Member States.**

UK v Council (The Working Time Directive) (Case C-84/94) 1996

The Council adopted Directive 93/104 based on Art.118a of the EC Treaty (harmonisation of health and safety in the working environment), providing, inter alia, that average weekly working time should not exceed 48 hours, that there should be specified minimum rest periods and that workers should be entitled to four weeks' annual paid leave. The United Kingdom challenged the measure under Art.230 (ex 173), claiming that it should have been adopted under Art.100 (now Art.94), requiring a unanimous vote, rather than Art.118a (now, after amendment, Art.138), requiring a qualified majority vote, and that it contravened the principle of subsidiarity.

Held: (ECJ) The measure was properly adopted under Art.118a (except for the second sentence of Art.5, specifying Sunday for a rest day: annulled).

(2) The adoption of the directive was not inconsistent with the principle of subsidiarity. [1996] 3 C.M.L.R. 671.

Commentary

(1) Subsidiarity was introduced into the EC Treaty by the Maastricht Treaty. It represents a check on the powers of the EC institutions by creating a presumption in favour of action by the Member States in areas where the EC does not possess exclusive powers (e.g. competition policy, environmental protection, education, transport). Article 5 (ex 3b) EC incorporates the principle of proportionality by stating that action by the EC shall not exceed what is necessary to achieve the objectives of the Treaty. For further clarification of the principle, see the Protocol on Subsidiarity annexed to the EC Treaty by the ToA.

(2) In *UK v Council* the need to improve the existing level of health and safety of workers through the imposition of minimum requirements presupposed EC-wide action. There was no breach of the principle of proportionality in the Council's view that improvements in the health and safety of workers could not be achieved by less restrictive measures.

(3) The principle of subsidiarity is increasingly invoked as a ground where annulment is sought. (See Craig & De Burca pp.100–101) *UK v Council* (Case C-84/94); *Germany v EP*

and Council (Case C-233/94) (the Deposit Guarantee Directive case); *Germany v EP and Council* (Case C-376/98) (the Tobacco Advertising case); and *Netherlands v EP and Council* (Case C-377/98) (the Biotechnology Patents Directive case). In only one of these cases was the directive annulled (Tobacco Advertising), due to adoption on the wrong legal base. Thus breach of the principle of subsidiarity is yet to be successfully cited as a ground for annulment.

4. ENFORCEMENT OF EC LAW

Member States obligations under Article 10 (ex 5)

Key Principle: Member States must take all appropriate measures to ensure fulfilment of the obligations arising from the Treaty or from secondary legislation. They must facilitate the EC's tasks and abstain from measures which could jeopardise the objectives of the Treaty: Art.10 (ex 5).

Commission v Greece (Case 272/86) 1988
The Commission requested information from the Greek Government relating to cereal imports during enforcement proceedings under Art.226 (ex 169). Greece failed to supply information at both the informal and formal stages.

Held: (ECJ) Failure to supply the information amounted to a failure to facilitate the achievement of the EC's tasks under Art.10 (ex 5). [1988] E.C.R. 4875.

Commentary
Art.10 lies at the heart of the Member States' obligations to implement and apply EC law. It is directly effective and is frequently cited by the ECJ. See e.g. *Von Colson* (Case 14/83) (see p.10) and *Francovich* (Joined Cases C-6 & 9/90). As the EC lacks the mechanisms necessary to enforce EC law (with the exception of the power to fine under Art.228 (ex 171): see p.46 below) this obligation is transferred to the Member States under Art.10.

Actions under Article 226 (ex 169)

Key Principle: If the Commission considers that a Member State has failed to fulfil an obligation under the Treaty, it shall deliver a reasoned opinion on the matter after giving the state concerned the opportunity to submit its observations. If the state concerned does not comply with the opinion within the period laid down, the Commission may bring the matter before the ECJ: Art.226 (ex 169).

Key Principle: As the reasoned opinion sets out the scope of the judicial proceedings under Art.226 (ex 169), both sets of documents must be founded on the same grounds and submissions.

Commission v Italy (Case 31/69) 1970

The Commission informed the Italian Government by a letter dated July 12, 1986 that it had failed to comply with various regulations over refunds under the Common Agricultural Policy (CAP). In the reasoned opinion delivered in November 1968, the Commission found that Italy was in breach of the obligations under the Regulations. When proceedings were issued in the ECJ they included references to infringement of two regulations of June 1968 which had not been set out in the reasoned opinion.

Held: (ECJ) Even if the Member State concerned does not consider it necessary to avail itself of the opportunity to submit its observations, such an opportunity constitutes an essential guarantee under the Treaty and amounts to an essential procedural requirement in proceedings under Art.226 (ex 169). The alleged failure deriving from the regulations of June 1968 must be excluded from the proceedings. [1970] E.C.R. 25.

Commentary

(1) Art.226 (ex 169) provides a two-stage mechanism (the administrative and judicial stages) for the Commission to bring proceedings against a Member State which has infringed an obligation under EC law. During the administrative stage the Commission sends a letter setting out the breach and negotiates with the state in question. If the matter is unresolved the Commission may issue a reasoned opinion.

(2) The reasoned opinion must contain "a coherent statement of reasons which led the Commission to believe that the state in question has failed to fulfil an obligation under the Treaty": *Commission v Italy (Pigmeat)* (Case 7/61). It must also specify the action required to remedy the breach and any period for implementation.

(3) Non-compliance with the opinion entitles the Commission to start formal proceedings in the ECJ (the judicial stage). The decision to proceed is a matter for the discretion of the Commission: *Star Fruit v Commission* (Case 247/87).

(4) While there has been a significant increase in the number offormal letters of notice of infringements (1,209 letters in 1993 compared with 960 in 1990), more than half the cases are settled before the reasoned opinion is issued. About 70 cases a year reach the ECJ for decision under the formal procedure.

Key Principle: **In deciding to issue a reasoned opinion, the Commission acts as a college.**

Commission v Germany (Case C-191/95)

The Commission brought enforcement proceedings against Germany under Art.226 (ex 169) for a declaration that, by failing to impose penalties on companies which do not disclose their annual accounts (as required by various EC directives), Germany was in breach of EC law. At the time that the Commission decided to pursue proceedings in the ECJ, it had the facts of the case but not the text of the reasoned opinion before it.

Held: (ECJ) The Commission's decision to issue a reasoned opinion and to bring an action for failure to fulfil obligations was the subject of collective deliberation by the college of commissioners. The college must be able to decide on the basis of the relevant information, though it need not decide on the final wording of the Act (normally an administrative step). The action was found to be admissible. [1998] E.C.R. I-000.

Key Principle: **Force majeure is no defence to an action under Art.226 (ex 169).**

Commission v Italy (Case 101/84) 1986

Italy failed to submit statistical returns to the Commission from 1979 in relation to the carriage of goods contrary to Directive 78/546. The Italian Government put forward a defence of force majeure, claiming that it had been unable to comply following the destruction in a bomb blast of the vehicle register at the Data Processing Centre of the Ministry of Transport.

Held: (ECJ) While the bomb attack may originally have amounted to force majeure, the ensuing difficulties had only lasted for a certain time. The administration had failed to exercise due diligence to replace the equipment and collect the data. The Italian Government could not, therefore, rely on the event to justify its continuing failure to comply [1985] E.C.R. 1077.

Commentary

Unless there has been a procedural flaw in the Commission's action, defences to actions in the ECJ under Art.226 have rarely succeeded. This is due to the strength of the Commission's case when proceedings reach the judicial stage, as complaints that are not well founded are normally resolved at the administrative stage.

Key Principle: Practical difficulty in implementation is not a defence to enforcement proceedings.

Commission v UK (Case 128/78) 1979

Regulation 1463/70 provided for the installation of tachographs (to record rest periods and duration of driving) in vehicles used to carry passengers and goods on roads. It was due for implementation by January 1, 1976. The United Kingdom introduced a voluntary scheme to record the information and stated that it did not intend to implement the Regulation fully for economic, industrial and practical considerations.

Held: (ECJ) Difficulties of implementation cannot be accepted as a justification. In permitting Member States to profit from membership of the EC, the Treaty places on them the obligation to observe its rules. For a state to break the rules unilaterally is a breach of the principle of solidarity under Art.10 (ex 5). [1979] E.C.R. 419.

Commentary

(1) Italy unsuccessfully argued that it should have a defence to proceedings arising out of non-implementation of a directive due to its frequent changes of government which prevented the adoption of national legislation: *Commission v Italy* (Case 28/81). Italy has been the most persistent offender in terms of Art.226 (ex 169) actions. It has sought to remedy the problem by passing a statute that annually transposes all EC directives (verbatim) into national law.

(2) Ireland stated in response to enforcement proceedings arising from its failure to transpose a directive on the interoperability of the trans-European high-speed rail system,

that no high speed train was in operation at the time or would be in the foreseeable future. The ECJ considered the lack of a highspeed train to be irrelevant, pointing out the fact that if an activity referred to in a directive does not exist in a particular Member State, this cannot release the state from its obligation to ensure that the directive is properly transposed.

(3) If the ECJ finds that the state is in breach it will require the defaulting state to take the necessary steps to comply with the judgment: Art.228 (ex 171). After amendment of Art.228 by the Maastricht Treaty, if the state concerned does not comply, the Commission may issue a reasoned opinion after following a repetition of the procedure under Art.226 (ex 169) specifying the points of non-compliance. Non-compliance with the reasoned opinion entitles the Commission to bring the case before the ECJ, which may impose a lump sum or penalty payment.

Key Principle: **If a Member State fails to comply with a judgment of the ECJ following enforcement proceedings it may impose a lump sum or periodical payment on it: under Art.228 (ex 171).**

Commission v Greece (Case C-387/97) 2000
The Commission applied to the ECJ for a declaration under Art.228 and for imposition of a daily periodical penalty, following Greece's failure to comply with a judgment against it of April 7, 1992 in Case C-45/91. The judgment required Greece to draw up and implement plans to dispose of toxic and dangerous waste under several environmental directives.

Held: (1) By failing to take the necessary measures to dispose of waste, Greece had not implemented the judgment in Case C-45/91 and had failed to fulfil its obligations under Art.171 of the Treaty.

(2) The basic criteria which must be taken into account in order to ensure that penalty payments have coercive force and EC law is applied uniformly and effectively are: the duration of the infringement, its degree of seriousness and the ability of the Member States to pay. In applying

these criteria, regard should be made in particular to the effects which failure to comply has on public and private interests and to the urgency of getting the Member State to fulfil its obligations.

Commentary

(1) The ECJ considered that a periodical payment was best suited to the circumstances of the case and imposed a payment of €20,000 for each day of delay in implementing the necessary measures to comply with the judgment in Case C-45/91, from the date of the present judgment until full compliance.

(2) In *Commission v France* (Case C-304/02) the ECJ imposed both a lump sum and penalty payment at the same time. The case arose out of an earlier judgment in 1991 against France (Case C-64/88) for infringement of fisheries conservation measures. The Court found that Art.228 did not preclude the imposition of both types of penalties, in particular where the breach had continued for a long time and was inclined to persist. As a result. France was ordered to pay a lump sum of €20,000,000 and a penalty payment of €57,651,250 for each period of six months from delivery of the present judgment until full compliance with the judgment in Case C-64/88.

Key Principle: **The ECJ may prescribe the necessary interim measures in any cases before it: Art.241 (ex 184).**

Commission v UK (Case 221/89R) 1989
For facts, see Ch.1, p.7.

Held: (ECJ) The United Kingdom must suspend the offending provisions of the Merchant Shipping Act 1988, pending the determination of the proceedings under Art.226 (ex 169).

Commentary
Applications for interim relief are normally heard before the President of the ECJ, who has the discretion to refer cases to the full court, if necessary.

Actions between Member States under Art.227 (ex 170)

Key Principle: Where a Member State considers that another Member State is in breach of EC law it may bring the matter before the ECJ if it has put the case before the Commission which has not acted within three months of the reasoned opinion: Art.227 (ex 170).

France v UK (Re Fishing Net Mesh Sizes) (Case 141/78)
France complained to the Commission about United Kingdom measures on fishing net mesh sizes. When the Commission did not proceed in the ECJ under Art.226 (ex 169) France brought the matter before the ECJ under Art.227 (ex 170).

Held: (ECJ) The United Kingdom was in breach of EC law on fishing net mesh sizes. [1979] E.C.R. 2923.

Commentary
Member States prefer to leave the resolution of their disputes with other states in the hands of the Commission, thus avoiding direct confrontation. Article 227 (ex 170) provides a mechanism for an aggrieved state to pursue its action directly against another state when the Commission has not acted on a reasoned opinion.

Although proceedings have been commenced in a few other cases under Art.227, France v UK is the only one resulting in an order against another state. The ECJ rejected an application by Belgium against Spain over a Spanish requirement that wine labelled "Rioja" must be bottled in the region of production: *Belgium v Spain* (Case C-388/95).

Specific enforcement proceedings

Actions under Article 88 (ex 93(2)) on illegal state aids

Key Principle: The Commission may issue a decision requiring a state to change or abolish illegal state aid within a specified time. Failure to comply entitles the Commission or any interested state to bring the matter before the ECJ: Art.88 (ex 93(2)).

British Aerospace and Rover Group Holdings Plc v Commission (Case C-292/90) 1992
The Commission had issued a decision requiring the United Kingdom Government to recover payments considered to be illegal state aid made to the Rover Group before its take-over by British Aerospace. While the aid to Rover to absorb debts had been approved by the Commission, provided no further aid was granted, additional unauthorised financial concessions ("sweeteners" of £44.4 million) were made by the United Kingdom Government to British Aerospace. British Aerospace and Rover sought annulment of part of the decision in the ECJ.

Held: (ECJ) If the Commission considered that the United Kingdom had not complied with conditions in the decision and had paid further aid, it should have instituted proceedings directly against the United Kingdom under Art.88 (ex 93(2)), and given notice to the parties concerned to submit their comments. The decision was annulled in relation to the requirement to recover the additional payment of £44.4 million. [1992] E.C.R. I-493.

Commentary
After the judgment the Commission reopened proceedings on a proper basis under Art.88 (ex 93(2)), treating the payment as aid.
    An out-of-court settlement was reached with the United Kingdom Government, as a result of which the sum was agreed to be repaid with interest.

Challenge under Article 298 (ex 225) to the use of expedited procedures

Key Principle: **Where it considers that a state is acting improperly, the Commission may challenge the action of a state which has brought expedited proceedings under Art.296 (ex 223) or 297 (ex 224): Art.298 (ex 225).**

Commission v Greece (Case C-120/94R) 1994
The Commission sought interim relief in relation to the closure by Greece of its border with the former Yugoslavian Republic of Macedonia, pending the hearing of the main action (Case C-120/94).

Held: (ECJ) Interim relief was refused. The ECJ considered that the interpretation of Arts 296–298 (ex 223–225) was uncer-

tain and did not accept that there was an urgent prima facie case
for relief. [1994] E.C.R. I-3037.

Commentary

Member States may derogate from the Treaty under Arts 296 (ex
223) and 297 (ex 224): (a) to protect essential interests of their
security connected with production and trade in arms, munitions
and war material; (b) where there is serious internal disturbance
affecting the maintenance of law and order; and (c) in the event of
a serious balance of payments crisis. Member States must co-
operate closely with the Commission to avoid improper use of
these powers.

5. JUDICIAL REVIEW OF THE ACTS OF THE EC INSTITUTIONS

Action for annulment under Article 230 (ex 173)

Reviewable acts

Key Principle: **The ECJ may review the legality of acts adopted jointly by the EP and the Council, of acts of the Council, of the Commission and of the European Central Bank (ECB), and of acts of the EP intended to produce legal effects vis-à-vis third parties: Art.230 (ex 173).**

Parti Ecologise ("Les Verts") v EP (Case 294/83) 1986
Prior to amendment by the Maastricht Treaty, Art.173 (now 230) did not expressly provide that acts of the EP may be challenged.

Les Verts (the Green Party) sought under Art.173 to challenge the allocation of funds by the Bureau of the EP to fight the 1984 European elections.

Held: (ECJ) An action for annulment may lie against measures adopted by the EP where they are intended to produce legal effects vis-à-vis third parties. The allocation was annulled. [1986] E.C.R. 1339.

Commentary
The decision in *"Les Verts"* has been incorporated verbatim in the amended version of Art.230(1) (ex 173(1)), reflecting the increased involvement of the EP in the decision-making process. See the pre-TEU decision in *Luxembourg v EP* (Case 230/81), [1983] E.C.R. 255, in which the ECJ annulled a resolution of the EP to move its seat from Luxembourg to Brussels, based on an action under the ECSC Treaty which recognised the power to review acts of the EP.

Key Principle: **The ECJ will look at the substance rather than the form of a measure to determine whether it is intended to have legal effect.**

Cimenteries v Commission (Noordwijk's Cement Accord) (Cases 8(11/66) 1967

Various undertakings enjoyed exemption from fines under a regulation in relation to competition. They were exposed to penalties when the Commission changed its practice in a notice sent out in a registered letter.

Held: (ECJ) (1) The measure affected the undertakings' interests by changing their legal position.

(2) It was not a mere opinion but a decision intended to produce legal effects and must be considered a reviewable act. [1967] E.C.R. 75.

Commentary

(1) In *Cimenteries* and "*Les Verts*" the ECJ has recognised a category of reviewable acts known as "acts sui generis", not appearing in Art.249 (ex 189) (which refers specifically to regulations, directives and decisions).

(2) Other examples of reviewable acts include:

    (a) discussions of guidelines before the signing of the European Road Transport Agreement: *Commission v Council* (Re Erta) (Case 22/70);

    (b) a code of conduct issued by the Commission concerning the administration of the Structural Fund: *France v Commission* (Case C-303/90).

(3) Applicants, both privileged and non-privileged, must bring a claim for annulment within two months of publication of the measure, or of notification to the applicant, or of the day on which the applicant had knowledge of the measure (if not notified): Art.230(3) (ex 173(3)). Outside the time limit it may be easier to bring a challenge under Art.241 (ex 184) (see p.63).

Key Principle: **Certain "acts" may be so seriously affected by defects of form or procedure that they are non-existent and incapable of annulment.**

Commission v BASF A.G. (Case C-137/92 P) 1992

The original text of a decision imposing fines on various chemical companies had been altered after its adoption. Also, it had only been adopted in three of the official languages, leaving it to the Commissioner to adopt versions in the other languages. The CFI considered the decision to be so defective in form as to be nonexistent. The Commission appealed to the ECJ.

Held: (ECJ) The decision was defective but not sufficiently tainted by irregularity as to be non-existent. The original measure was annulled. A measure would be non-existent where it was "tainted by an irregularity whose gravity is so obvious that it cannot be tolerated by the Community legal order". [1994] E.C.R. I-2555.

Commentary

(1) Acts of the EC institutions are presumed to be lawful. Only in exceptional circumstances will an act be found to be non-existent.

(2) Other, less exceptional, examples of non-reviewable acts include:

(a) a reasoned opinion under Art.226 (ex 169): *Commission v Italy* (Pigmeat) (Case 7/61);

(b) "comfort" letters issued by the Commission in competition cases, stating that an undertaking is not in breach of Art.85(1) or is exempt: *Lancôme v Etos B.V.* (Perfumes) (Case 99/79).

Locus standi: the right to challenge

Key Principle: **Member States, the Council and the Commission may bring actions for annulment before the ECJ on specified grounds. The EP and the ECB (after amendment by the TEU) may bring actions on the same grounds for the purpose of protecting their prerogatives: Art.230(2) and (3) (ex 170(2) and (3)).**

EP v Council ("Chernobyl") **(Case C-70/88) 1990**
The EP challenged the legal basis of a Council regulation on the permitted level of radioactive contamination in foodstuffs following the Chernobyl explosion.

Held: (ECJ) The ECJ shall have jurisdiction in actions brought by the EP or the ECB for the purpose of protecting their prerogatives. [1990] E.C.R. I-2041.

Commentary

(1) Prior to amendment by the Maastricht Treaty, Art.173 (now 230) did not explicitly recognise any entitlement by the EP to seek annulment. The *"Chernobyl"* decision partly over-ruled an earlier decision in *EP v Council ("Comitology")* (Case 302/87) in which the ECJ had ruled that the EP could not challenge under (old) Art.173 but only under Art.175 (now 232). The Maastricht Treaty amended Art.230(3) in line with the decision in Chernobyl. As a result, the EP, ECB and Court of Auditors were permitted to bring a challenge in order to protect their prerogative (normally arising in relation to a claim that a measure had been adopted on an incorrect legal base). The Treaty of Nice further amended Art.230(3) to place the EP on a par with the Council and Commission. As a result, only the ECB and Court of Auditors are limited to challenges where there is a threat to their prerogative.

(2) The Member States and EC institutions are known as "privileged" applicants as they do not have to show that a measure is addressed to them or otherwise concerns them directly.

(3) It is more difficult for non-privileged applicants (natural or legal persons) to establish locus standi. An individual may only challenge:
   (a) a decision addressed to himself (e.g. a competition decision by the Commission);
   (b) a decision in the form of regulation (i.e. a measure equivalent to a decision);
   (c) a regulation or decision addressed to another person which is of direct and individual concern to himself: Art.230(4).

Key Principle: **Only decisions or measures equivalent to decisions may be challenged.**

International Fruit N.V. (No.1) v Commission (Cases 41–44/70) The applicant sought to challenge a regulation that prescribed the number of import licences for a particular period on the basis of previous applications.

Held: (ECJ) As the regulation applied to a finite number of people identifiable from their previous applications it had the character of a decision and could be challenged. [1971] E.C.R. 411.

Commentary
A regulation applies generally to categories of persons whereas a decision (or measure with the character of a decision) binds those to whom it is addressed, i.e. named or identifiable individuals. Some regulations are hybrid in that they apply generally but operate as decisions for certain individuals.

Key Principle: **If the measure is not addressed to the applicant, it must be of direct and individual concern to him.**

Toepfer K.G. v Commission (Cases 106 & 107/63) 1965
The applicant, an importer of maize, sought an import licence from the German Government. The German Government refused, seeking authorisation from the Commission for the safeguard measures it had taken. A Commission decision addressed to Germany approved the safeguard measures and the Government's refusal to grant all existing applicants a licence.

Held: As the decision affected only existing applicants it was of individual concern to the applicant. The decision was annulled. [1965] E.C.R. 405.

Plaumann & Co v Commission (Case 25/62)
P, a major importer of clementines, sought to challenge a Commission decision addressed to the German Government refusing to allow the Government to reduce the duty on clementines imported from outside the EC.

Held: To establish individual concern the applicant must show that he is affected by the decision as a result of factors particularly relevant to him, not because he is a member of a class affected by the measure. The application was inadmissible. [1963] E.C.R. 95.

Commentary
(1) The difference between the locus standi of the applicants in *Toepfer* and *Plaumann* is that T could be identified as a member of a closed class of persons affected by the decision whereas P could not. (Anyone could import clementines.)

(2) See also *Spijker Kwasten N.V. v Commission* (Case 231/82):
    A Commission decision to allow a Dutch import ban on
    Chinese brushes could not be challenged by a previous
    import licence holder. Note in addition *UPA* (Case
    C-50/00P) on p.58.

(3) This restrictive approach was recently followed by the ECJ
    in *Greenpeace Council v Commission* (Case C-321/95P),
    upholding the decision of the CFI to refuse to recognise
    locus standi. The applicants were local residents and an
    environmental group opposed to the building of a power
    station. The basis of the ECJ's decision was that the
    applicants had only an indirect interest in the decision to
    provide financial assistance in the building of the power
    station.

(4) In a few cases the ECJ has demonstrated a liberal approach
    to locus standi. In *Piraiki-Patraiki* (Case 11/82) Greek
    producers of cotton were found to be individually con-
    cerned in a Commission decision, due mainly to the obliga-
    tion in the Greek Act of Accession to take such interests into
    account. See also *Sofrimport v Commission* (Case
    C-152/88): Importers with goods in transit could challenge
    a regulation that had to take account of their interests.

Key Principle: **The fact that a general legislative measure
applies to traders in a general way does not necessarily
prevent individual traders from being individually concerned.**

Codorniu v Council (Case C-309/89) 1993

C sought to challenge a Regulation reserving the word
"crémant" for high-quality sparkling wines from specific
regions in France and Luxembourg. C was a major producer of
similar sparkling wines in Spain where it held a trade mark, and
the largest producer of wines labelled "crémant" in the EU.

Held: (ECJ) The applicant was individually concerned because
the reservation to producers in France and Luxembourg inter-
fered with C's intellectual property rights. [1994] E.C.R. I-1853.

Commentary

(1) This decision departs from the previous case law of the ECJ
    in that there was no suggestion that the Regulation had been
    adopted with the applicant in mind.

(2) Jurisdiction to hear Art.230 (ex 173) applications brought by non-privileged applicants passed to the CFI in August 1993. So far the CFI has followed the pre-*Codorniu*, more restrictive approach of the ECJ in refusing to accept that a claim to locus standi could be based on a disadvantageous competitive position. See *Campo Edro Industrial v Council* (Case T-472/93) in which a regulation gave aid in sugar pricing to producers of sugar from cane and beet but not to isoglucose producers. Despite being the sole Spanish producers of isoglucose, the applicants were denied locus standi to challenge the regulation. A similarly restrictive approach was taken in *CSR Pampryl v Commission* (Case T-114/99). Here a long-standing cider producer who had sold cider under various names including the indication "Pays d'Auge" sought to challenge a regulation which registered "Pays d'Auge" as a protected designation. The applicant failed to establish that the use of the geographical name over which it claimed a right stemmed from a specific right granted at national or EC law before the regulation and which had been adversely affected by that regulation.

(3) The CFI in February 2002 dismissed as inadmissible an application by 70 MEPs to annul a decision by the EP on amendments to its Rules of Procedure following the Interinstitutional Agreement of May 1999 between the EP, the Council and the Commission on internal investigations by the European Anti-Fraud Office. The CFI considered that there were no factors enabling individual MEPs to be distinguished individually. As the measure affected the applicants in the same way as all other MEPs, the inadmissibility of the action did not create inequality between the applicants and other MEPs.

(4) For a brief two-month period it looked as if a new and moreliberal approach to standing was developing. In May 2002 the CFI departed from the ECJ's approach in a surprise decision. In *Jégo-Quéré* (Case T-177/01) a French fishing company, Jégo-Quéré et Cie ('JQ') had fished for some time off Ireland using nets with a mesh size which was prohibited as a result of Commission Regulation 1162/2001. JQ sought to challenge the Regulation, clearly a measure of general application, under Art.230 in the CFI. The CFI upheld the action as admissible, referring to the need to avoid depriving JQ of the right to an effective remedy under Arts 6 and 13 of the ECHR. The CFI considered that

neither indirect review under Art.234 nor an action for damages based on the non-contractual liability of the EC institutions was a satisfactory route. The best solution was to reconsider the established caselaw of the Court on standing. It proposed that a non-privileged individual applicant should be regarded as individually concerned by a measure of general application if it "affects his legal position in a manner which is both definite and immediate, by restricting his rights or by imposing obligations on him".

(5) The ECJ in July 2002 reverted to a more traditional, restrictive view on standing in *Unión de Pequenos Agricultores* (UPA) (Case C-50/00P), refusing to depart from previous caselaw, despite support for liberalisation expressed by Advocate General Jacobs. The applicant, UPA, a trade association in Spain, had sought to challenge part of Regulation 1638/98 on the common organisation of the market in olive oil. The ECJ held that standing continued to be determined according to the rules in the Plaumann decision and upheld the decision of the CFI that UPA was not individually concerned and so could not challenge the Regulation. Individuals who lack standing may, the ECJ pointed out, plead invalidity before the ECJ under Art.241. Alternatively, an action may be brought before the national courts who may be asked to make a reference to the ECJ under Art.234.

Responsibility for ensuring effective judicial protection rests with the Member States. The ECJ refused to intervene if such protection were absent. Any change to the rules on standing may only come through amendment to the wording of Art.230.

(6) The hard line on standing was maintained by the CFI in January 2003 against tobacco companies from the Philip Morris and Reynolds Groups: *Philip Morris International* (Joined Cases T-377/00, T-379/00, etc.). The cases involved decisions to bring proceedings before the US courts in connection with allegations that the cigarette companies were involved in smuggling cigarettes into the EC for distribution. The applicants sought to challenge the decisions to proceed. The CFI ruled that the applications were inadmissible, repeating the formula in UPA that it was not the function of the Court to usurp the authority of the Community deriving from the Treaty.

(7) Under the Constitutional Treaty (Article III-270) any natural or legal person will be empowered to challenge a regulatory act which is of direct and individual concern to him or her and which does not entail implementing measures. This amendment would, on the face of it, improve the standing of non-privileged applicants (in the event of full ratification of the Treaty). However, its potential remains subject to interpretation by the European Courts, which may adhere to the conservative line on standing in *UPA*.

Key principle: **An individual is only directly concerned in a measure where its implementation leaves no discretion to the addressees.**

Regione Siciliana v Commission (Case T-341/02) 2004
The Commission provided financil assistance to Italy from the Regional Development Fund for the construction of a motorway in Sicily between Messina and Palermo. It issued a decision addressed to the Republic of Italy ending the assistance. The authority responsible for implementing the project, the Region of Sicily, sought to challenge the decision under Art.230.

Held: (CFI) As the national authorities had discretion in implementing the contested measure, the Region of Sicily lacked direct interest in the proceedings and so lacked standing to bring a challenge.

Commentary
An applicant will only be able to establish that a measure is of direct and individual concern where it affects his legal position and where its implementation flows automatically from the EC measure without the need for the adoption of further rules. This decision is currently under appeal to the ECJ (Case C-417/04P).

Grounds for challenge

Key Principle: **A measure may be challenged under Art.230 if an essential procedural requirement is infringed.**

Roquette Frères S.A. v Council (Case 138/79) 1980
The Council sent the EP a draft regulation fixing a quota for isoglucose producers for consultation in March 1979, asking for

its views during April, so that the measure could be adopted by July. This would only have been possible if the EP had convened a special session but no such request was made by the Council or Commission. The measure was adopted by the Council in June 1979, with reference in the Preamble to the fact that the EP had been "consulted". R, a member of a closed group of isoglucose producers, sought to challenge the regulation.

Held: (ECJ) Failure to consult the EP, as required under Art.43(2) of the Treaty, was a breach of an essential procedural requirement. The regulation was annulled. [1980] E.C.R. 3393.

Commentary

(1) Wrongly identifying the legal basis of a measure may lead to failure to consult the EP (See Ch.2).

(2) Failure to specify the legal basis of a measure may also be regarded as breach of an essential procedural requirement: *Commission v Council* (Case 45/86), as may failure to state the reasons for a decision: *Germany v Commission (Re Tariff Quotas on Wine)* (Case 24/62).

(3) A measure may also be challenged under Art.230 on groundsof lack of competence (similar to ultra vires in English law) (See, for example, *Germany v EP and Council* (Case C-367/98), the Tobacco Advertising case, in which the ECJ annulled a decision of the CFI due to the Commission's lack of competence to impose a general ban on tobacco advertising under Art.95 (ex 100a), 47(2) (ex 57(2)) and 55(ex 66), infringement of the EC Treaty or any rule relating to its application, or misuse of power.

(4) There is a time limit of two months from the date of the decision within which to bring a challenge under Art.120. In *Pitsiorlas v Council* and ECB (Case T-3/00) (under appeal Case C-193/01P) the CFI stated that, in exceptional circumstances, an excusable error may have the effect of making the applicant not out of time. There were no such circumstances in this case and the application was held to be inadmissible.

Key Principle: **A measure may be annulled where it is in breach of a general principle of EC law.**

Transocean Marine Paint Association v EC Commission (Case 17/74) 1974

The Commission issued a measure in relation to the renewal of an exemption from the competition rules policy without providing an opportunity for the members of the Association to be heard. The Association argued that the measure should be annulled because it had been denied a hearing.

Held: (ECJ) A person whose interests are affected by a decision by a public authority such as the Commission considering an exemption must be given an opportunity to submit his observations. The offending part of the measure was annulled. [1974] E.C.R. 1063.

Commentary

(1) This case provides an example of the ECJ's adoption of a general principle from the domestic law of the Member States: in this case, the United Kingdom (audi alterem partem). Infringement of a rule to the Treaty's application is interpreted liberally by the ECJ to cover any general principle of law, whether in international law, in the domestic legal systems of the Member States or in the general principles recognised by the ECJ (see Ch.3).

(2) Before and after the terrorist attacks of September 11, 2001, the UN Security Council adopted a number of resolution calling on all UN Member States to freeze the funds or other financial resources controlled by the Taliban, Usama bin Laden and the Al-Qaeda network. The resolutions were put into effect within the EU by various Council regulations, with the persons concerned listed in an annex. Derogation may be granted by the Member States on humanitarian grounds. Several persons and entities sought annulment of the regulations in the CFI which has recently given judgment in the first two cases. The Court held that the EC is competent to order the freezing of individual assets as part of the fight against international terrorism. Although the EC is not a member of the UN, it must consider itself bound by the UN Charter. The Court found that, in so far as they are required by the UN Security Council, the measures fall mostly outside the scope of judicial review and do not infringe universally recognized human rights including the right to property, the right of defence and the right of effective judicial review:

Kadi v Council and Commission (Case T-315/01); Yusuf, etc. v Council and Commission (Case T-306/01).

Action for inactivity under Article 232 (ex 175)

Key Principle: **If the EP, Council or Commission fails to act on an infringement of the Treaty, the Member States and other institutions of the EC may bring an action before the ECJ to have the failure established: Art.232 (ex 175).**

EP v Council (Case 13/83) 1985
The EP sought to challenge the failure of the Council to implement a common transport policy under Art.74 (now 70) and to reach a decision on 16 Commission proposals on transport.

Held: (ECJ) While there was no enforceable obligation to implement a common transport policy under Art.231 (ex 174), the Council was required to act to implement the freedoms expressed in Arts 71 (ex 75), 49 (ex 59), 41 (ex 50) and 51 (ex 61) within the transitional periods (end of 1961). To be enforceable, obligations must be sufficiently defined to allow the ECJ to establish whether failure to adopt them is lawful.

Commentary
This obligation mirrors that in Art.230 (ex 173). Rules on locus standi are similar, with the EC institutions in a privileged position, relative to individuals. Article 232 (ex 175) was amended by the Maastricht Treaty to include the EP and the ECB, as in Art.230.

Key Principle: **An individual may bring proceedings under Art.232 (ex 175) where an institution has failed to address to him or her an act other than a recommendation or opinion.**

Bethell v Commission (Case 246/81) 1982
Lord Bethell sought to force the Commission to apply the competition rules against various European airlines. As this sector was outside Reg.17, Lord Bethell had no entitlement to insist that the Commission carry out an investigation.

Held: The applicant was not directly and individually concerned and could not challenge the Commission's inaction under Art.232 (ex 175), nor its refusal to act under Art.230 (ex 173). [1982] E.C.R. 2277.

Commentary
No action may be brought under Art.232 (ex 175) unless the institution has first been called upon to act. It has two months in which to act or define its position, after which the applicant has a further two months in which to bring an action. A successful action under either Art.232 or 230 requires the institution to take the necessary steps to implement the judgment: Art.233 (ex 176). There are no sanctions for non-compliance.

Indirect challenge under Article 241 (ex 184)

Key Principle: **Despite the expiry of the time limit under Art.230(5) (ex 173(5)) (that is, two months from the date of adoption) any party may plead that a regulation is inapplicable on the grounds set out in Art.230(2) (ex 173(2))**

Italy v Council and Commission (Case 32/65) 1966
Italy brought proceedings under Art.230 (ex 173) to annul a regulation and indirectly challenged two further regulations under Art.241 (ex 184). The Commission raised the issue of whether a Member State may make an indirect challenge.

Held: (ECJ) As the regulations were not relevant to the issue in question the challenge under Art.241 (ex 184) was dismissed. [1966] E.C.R. 389.

Commentary

(1) The ECJ did not rule on the entitlement of a Member State to make an indirect challenge under Art.241 (ex 184).

(2) Art.241 (ex 184) applies only to regulations. However, it is substance not form that indicates the true character of a measure. (See *Simmenthal v Commission* (Case 92/78) in which the ECJ held that a general notice of invitation to tender was normative in character and thus capable of indirect challenge under Art.241.

(3) The effect of a successful challenge under Art.241 will lead to the regulation in question being declared inapplicable and any subsequent measure void.

6. LIABILITY OF THE EC INSTITUTIONS

Non-contractual Liability

Key Principle: **The EC must, in accordance with the general principles common to the laws of the Member States, make good any damage caused by its institutions or by its servants in performance of their duties (Art.288(2) (ex 215(2)).**

Lütticke v Commission (Case 4/69) 1966
L sued the Commission for damages under Art.288(2) (ex 215(2)), claiming that it had failed to require the German Government to change a disputed provision of national law. Under the German measure in question, L was obliged to pay taxes, which he alleged contravened EC law.

Held: (ECJ) There was no wrongful act or omission. The Commission had done all that it could in negotiating with the German Government. Non-contractual (tortious) liability is established under Art.288 where there is:

(a) a wrongful act or omission by an EC institution or its servants;

(b) damage to the applicant;

(c) a causal connection between the wrongful act or omission and the damage. [1971] E.C.R. 325.

Commentary

(1) *Lütticke* establishes that a claim for damages under Art.288(2) (ex 215(2)) is an independent action. It departs from the previous approach of the ECJ in *Plaumann* (see Ch.5) that annulment proceedings must be brought (under Art.173, 175 or 184) before a claim may be pursued under Art.215(2).

(2) Under Art.235 (ex 178) the ECJ has jurisdiction in compensation claims under Art.288(2) (ex 215(2)). Jurisdiction was transferred to the CFI in September 1993.

(3) In *New Europe Consulting and Brown v Commission* (Case T-231/97) the claim arose out of the sending of a fax by the Commission to a number of co-ordinators under the EC

PHARE programme alleging irregularities by the applicants. The applicants, a consultancy chosen to implement a programme, claimed that the Commission should compensate them for the harm suffered as a result of sending the fax. The CFI considered that the Commission should have held an enquiry into the alleged irregularities. It held that the three requirements of *Lütticke* were established: a wrongful act by the Commission, damage (in the form of harm to the image of the applicants) and a causal link between the breach and the damage. The Commission was ordered to pay compensation of €125,000.

(4) In *Cantina sociale di Dolianova v Commission* (Case T-166/98) the loss arose as a result of the Commission's failure to provide a scheme to pay compensation to the applicants for the preventive distillation for the wine. The CFI decided that the principle of non-discrimination and prohibition of unjustified enrichment had been infringed. Such breaches were seen as sufficiently serious and led to a rare finding against the Commission.

(5) Unlike non-contractual liability, there is no specific set of rules governing breach of contract under EC law. Under Art.288(1) (ex 215(1)) the contractual liability of the EC institutions is governed by the law applicable to the contract in question.

Key Principle: **Unusual and special damage must be established before the EC may incur for a lawful act.**

Dorsch Consult Ingenieurgesellschaft mbH (Case C-239/99 P)2000

The applicant entered into a contract in 1975 with the government of Iraq to organise and supervise the construction of a highway in Iraq. In August 1990, following the invasion of Kuwait by Iraq, the Security Council of the UN adopted a series of resolutions, including Resolution 661 (1990) which ordered an embargo to be placed on trade with Iraq. The Council of the EU responded immediately by adopting Regulation 2340/90 to that effect. The Iraqi government froze all assets and rights of companies trading with Iraq where those companies were based in countries covered by the embargo. The applicant, not having received payment from the Iraqi authorities for sums previously acknowledged, sought damages from the Council of the EU in the CFI in Case T-184/95. The claim was based on the submission that the loss was caused by the adoption of Regulation 2340/90 by the EC which in turn had led to the Iraqi action against companies such as the applicant. The application was dismissed. The applicant appealed to the ECJ.

Held: (ECJ) (upholding the decision of the CFI):

(1) It is necessary, where damages are claimed for a lawful or unlawful act by the EC institutions, to prove that the alleged damage is real and that a causal link exists between that act and the alleged damage. The damage could not be attributed to Regulation 2340/90, but to UN Resolution 661 (1990) imposing sanctions on Iraq.

(2) Where damages are claimed for a lawful act of the EC institutions, it is a precondition of liability that there is unusual and special damage. Iraq had to be regarded as a "high risk" country even before the invasion of Kuwait. As a result the damage suffered by the applicant did not exceed the economic risks inherent in the sector concerned.

Commentary

The ECJ noted that an applicant must produce evidence to show that it has exhausted all avenues and legal remedies open to it in order to recover its claim before the Court.

Key Principle: **Failure of administration ("faute de service") is a wrongful act or omission for which the EC is vicariously liable under Art.288(2).**

Richez-Parise v Commission (Case 19/69, etc.) 1969

Some members of staff of the Commission were given wrong information about pensions, as a result of which they decided to take early retirement. Although the Commission discovered the mistake it did not seek to correct the information. The officials sued the Commission under Art.288(2) (ex 215(2)).

Held: (ECJ) Even though the giving of the advice originally was not wrongful, failure to correct the information was a *"faute* *de service"*. The Commission was liable to compensate members of staff who had relied on its advice. [1970] E.C.R. 325.

Key Principle: **A negligent act by a servant is a wrongful act for which the EC will be vicariously liable provided it is performed in the course of his duties (*"faute de personne"*).**

Sayag v Leduc (Case 5/68) 1968
Sayag was an engineer employed by Euratom. While driving to visit an atomic plant in Belgium he injured someone in a road accident. The Belgian court made an Art.234 reference to the ECJ.

Held: (ECJ) Driving a motor vehicle is not an act performed in the course of duty unless it is necessary in an emergency or other exceptional circumstances. Euratom was not vicariously liable. [1969] E.C.R. 329.

Commentary
The distinction between *faute de service*, a fault in the operation of the system, and *faute personnelle*, a personal fault by an individual reflects French administrative law. Thus in EC law vicarious liability attaches to *faute de service* and to *faute personnelle* where the wrongful act is closely connected to the individual's duties (i.e. not a "frolic of one's own"). As in French law, the EC institutions may be vicariously liable for matters that would be considered maladministration in English law.

Liability for legislation: the "Schoppenstedt Formula"

Key Principle: **The EC is not liable in relation to a legislative measure involving choices of economic policy unless a sufficiently serious breach of a superior rule of law for the protection of the individual has occurred.**

Zuckerfabrik Schoppenstedt v Council (Case 5/71) 1971
The applicant, a sugar trader, sought compensation under Art.288(2) (ex 215(2)) for damage suffered as a result of a regulation, claiming that the measure infringed another regu-

lation and Art.34(3) (ex 40(3)) (the principle of non-discrimination under the CAP). The Council objected, claiming that the action would undermine the system of judicial review under Art.230 (ex 173).

Held: (ECJ) The ruling of the ECJ in *Lütticke* (see above) was approved and the application was declared admissible. However, the breach was not found to be "sufficiently flagrant". As a result the application failed. [1971] E.C.R. 975.

Commentary

(1) Most EC law involves choices of economic policy. It is the ECJ's responsibility to examine the acts of the institutions to determine when those acts should give rise to compensation to individuals. It is not intended that individuals should be protected from variations in the market.

(2) Although known as the "*Schoppenstedt* Formula", the principle stated above represents a reformulation by the ECJ in *Bayerische HNL v Council and Commission* (Joined Cases 83/76, etc.), approving the decision in *Schoppenstedt*. (See below.)

(3) The ECJ confirmed its adherence to the Schoppenstedt formula in Bergaderm (below). It restated the formula using slightly different wording.

Key Principle: **"Sufficiently serious breach" must be interpreted in the same way for the EC institutions as for the Member States.**

Laboratoires Pharmaceutiques Bergaderm and Goupil v Commission (Case C-352/98P) 2000

The applicant, in an appeal against a decision of the CFI, sought damages against the Commission for losses suffered as a result of a Commission directive on cosmetics. The directive prohibited the use of various substances thought to be possibly carcinogenic, one of which was used by the applicant (the only company to do so) in its sun-tan lotions. As a result, the applicant went into liquidation. The CFI dismissed the action and rejected the applicant's claim that the directive was an administrative rather than legislative act. The applicants appealed to the ECJ which upheld the decision of the CFI.

Held: (ECJ): EC law confers a right to damages where three conditions are met :

(1) the rule of law infringed must be intended to confer rights on individuals;

(2) the breach must be sufficiently serious;

(3) there must be a direct causal link between the breach of the obligation resting on the state and the damages sustained by the injured parties.

Commentary

(1) It is clear from the judgment of the ECJ in Bergaderm that it is not the nature of the measure which is significant but the degree of discretion enjoyed by the EC institution. Thus it makes no difference to an action in damages whether the act in question is legislative or administrative. See Hartley, *The Foundations of European Community Law* (5th ed.), p.467, "The test for determining whether there is discretion is whether the adoption of the act involves policy choices. It can hardly matter, however, whether these are economic, social or political."

(2) The test under Bergaderm to establish a sufficiently ser-iousbreach involving wide discretion is whether the EC institution manifestly and gravely disregarded the limits on its discretion.

Key Principle: **There must be a breach of a superior principle of law.**

CNTA v Commission (Case 74/74)
This case concerns the system for monetary compensation amounts (MCAs) payable to exporters under the CAP to com-pensate for fluctuations in exchange rates. CNTA entered into various export contracts before the system was abolished in France by the Commission, claiming to have based the contrac-tual prices on the MCAs. CNTA claimed damages for the losses arising from the ending of the scheme from the Commission.

Held: (ECJ) The regulation infringed the principle of legal certainty, in particular the principle of legitimate expectations. In the absence of overriding public interest the Commission had violated a superior rule of law by not taking transitional measures to protect the trader. However, as no actual loss had been suffered, no damages were awarded. [1975] E.C.R. 533.

Commentary
The wrongful act was the failure to give reasonable notice, not the adoption of the regulation (which was not declared invalid). Other general principles which have been invoked in damages claims include proportionality and equality. (See Ch.3).

Key Principle: **The breach must be sufficiently serious.**

Bayerische HNL v Council and Commission (Cases 83/76, etc.) 1978
In order to use up the skimmed milk powder "mountain" the Council adopted a regulation requiring animal feed producers to buy skimmed milk powder from EC intervention agencies. This was more expensive than soya, which had previously been used as feed. Some farmers brought actions in the national courts, leading to Art.234 references to the ECJ. Others claimed damages in the ECJ.

Held: (ECJ) (1) (Under Art.234 (ex 177)) The regulation was invalid because it infringed the principles of non-discrimination and proportionality. (2) (Under Art.215) There was a breach of a superior breach of law which was intended to protect the individual. However, the breach was not sufficiently serious; in a legislative field involving wide discretion, the EC is not liable unless there has been a manifest and grave breach. Thus damages were not available to the farmers. [1978] E.C.R. 1209.

Commentary
Despite the invalidity ruling under Art.234 (ex 177) it did not follow that the breach was serious enough to satisfy the *Schoppenstedt* Formula under Art.288 (ex 215).

Key Principle: **The rule of law must be intended for the protection of the individual.**

Kampffmeyer v Commission (Joined Cases 5/66, etc.) 1967

The applicants, German grain importers, applied to the German authorities for a licence to import grain from France. The German authorities refused, suspending imports. The Commission confirmed the decision. Under Regulation 19 such applications could only be refused if a serious disturbance of the market was threatened. The applicants challenged the Commission decision under Art.173 in the ECJ and also sued the German Government in the national courts.

Held: (ECJ) Although the rules of law in question were not of direct and individual concern to the applicant (under Art.230 (ex 173)), the protection of individual interests such as the applicant's was intended. The application was admissible. As there was no serious threat to the market, the Commission decision was unjustified (*faute de service*) and was annulled. [1967] E.C.R. 245.

Commentary

(1) A rule intended to benefit a class of persons may be found to benefit an individual.

(2) The ECJ deferred a decision on damages until the concurrent proceedings before the German courts were completed.

(3) The EC may not be liable where there is an overriding public interest. In *Mulder v Commission* (Joined Cases C-104/89 and 37/90) milk producers who had no quota due to lack of production in the year preceding their application were given a quota based on 60 per cent of production in the year before that.

Held: (ECJ) Although the quota decision was illegal because it infringed the principle of legitimate expectations, the Council had taken account of a higher public interest in fixing the rate, without gravely and manifestly disregarding the limits of its discretionary power. [1992] E.C.R. I-3061.

Damages

Key Principle: **Damages for loss of profits may be available against the EC institutions.**

CNTA v Commission (Case 74/74) 1975
See p.69.

Held: (ECJ) A firm is entitled to compensation for losses caused by currency speculation where this has been caused by the EC [1975] E.C.R. 533.

Commentary
The applicant was not in fact exposed to risk because its purchaser could pay in either French francs or American dollars. As the purchaser had paid in francs (with no exchange rate consequences) there was no actual loss. Traders cannot rely on the EC for protection against the operation of the market.

Key Principle: **An award of damages may be reduced by the contributory negligence of the applicant.**

Adams v Commission (Case 145/83) 1985
Stanley Adams was employed in Switzerland by the pharmaceutical company, Hoffman-La Roche. He handed over documents to the Commission, as a result of which the company was found to have infringed Art.86 and fined. Adams had requested confidentiality from the Commission, which failed to ensure that he was not identified from the documents. On returning to Switzerland from Italy where he had set up a business, Adams was arrested and charged with industrial espionage under Swiss law. Adams' wife committed suicide while her husband was in custody awaiting trial. Adams was convicted of industrial espionage and given a one-year's suspended sentence. He claimed that his credit-worthiness had been destroyed, leading to the failure of his business in Italy.

Held: (ECJ) The Commission was liable for breach of the principle of confidentiality and for failing to warn Adams of the risk of prosecution in Switzerland. The damages were reduced by one half due to Adams' carelessness in failing to inform the

Commission of his whereabouts and in returning to Switzerland despite the risk of prosecution. [1985] E.C.R. 3539.

Commentary

As there have been relatively few awards of damages made by the ECJ or CFI it is difficult to identify a set of principles from individual decisions, beyond stating that damages should not be too remote (*Lütticke*) and must be a sufficiently direct result of an unlawful act or omission by an EC institution (*Dumortier Fils S.A. v Council* (Joined Cases 64/76, etc.). Note the liberal limitation period (five years) for bringing a claim under Art.215(2) (Art.43 of the Statute of the Court), unlike the two month period for an annulment action under Art.230 (ex 173).

Concurrent Liability

Key Principle: **Where the national authority is primarily at fault the action should be brought in the national courts.**

Kampffmeyer v Commission (Cases 5/66, etc.) 1967
See p.71.

Held: (ECJ) The amount of damages awarded against the Commission could not be finalised until K had completed proceedings before the German courts.

Commentary

(1) The requirement to pursue a remedy in the national courts has been upheld in *Haegeman v Commission* (Case 96/71). There are problems arising from this approach as the scope or availability of a remedy may vary between Member States.

(2) The ECJ has not been consistent on the need to exhaust national remedies before proceeding in the ECJ (now in the CFI).

In *Krohn v Commission* (Case 175/84) it was held to be appropriate to bring an action in the ECJ rather than the national courts where the national authorities, on Commission instructions, had refused an import licence.

7. PRELIMINARY RULINGS

Preliminary rulings under Article 234 (ex 177)

Key Principle: Art.234 is essential for the Community character of the law established by the Treaty and has the object of ensuring that in all circumstances, EC law is given the same interpretation in all states of the Community.

Rheinmühlen-Düsseldorf v Einfuhr-und Vorratsstelle Getreide (Joined Cases 146 & 166/73) 1974

R, a German cereal exporter, unsuccessfully sought to rely on EC law in the Hessian Tax Court to obtain an export rebate. He appealed to the Federal Tax Court (Bundesfinanzhof) which quashed the decision of the lower court, holding that R was entitled to a rebate. The case was sent back to the Hessian Tax Court to decide certain points of fact. The Hessian Tax Court, although bound under German law by the decisions of the Federal Tax Court, refused to follow the decision of the higher court and referred several questions to the ECJ under Art.234 (ex 177). R appealed to the Federal Tax Court against the lower court's decision to make a reference. The Federal Tax Court then referred further questions to the ECJ to determine the extent of a lower court's powers to make a reference in such circumstances.

Held: (ECJ) The power of a lower court to make a reference cannot be abrogated by national law; the lower court must be free to refer if it considers that the higher court's ruling could lead to it giving a judgment contrary to EC law. [1974] E.C.R. 33.

Commentary

(1) Art.234 provides a mechanism which enables the ECJ to givepreliminary rulings on:

    (a) the interpretation of the EC Treaty;

    (b) the validity and interpretation of acts of the institutions of the EC Treaty and of the European Central Bank; and

    (c) the interpretation of the statutes of bodies established by an act of the Council.

(2) The procedure has been of great importance in the development of EC Law. As the EC Treaty is a framework (or "*traité cadre*") with little detail or definition, the ECJ has used the procedure to explain and clarify its provisions. The task of interpreting EC law has been described by Bingham J. in the High Court as involving the "creative process of supplying flesh to a spare and loosely constructed skeleton", *Customs and Excise v Samex*, 1983.

(3) The interpretations apply equally to all Member States, irrespective of the origin of any individual reference, thus ensuring uniformity of interpretation throughout the EC. Article 234 rulings are interlocutory rulings provided by the ECJ. After the question has been formulated by the national court, proceedings should be suspended pending the ruling. (This may take up to two years.) The national court should then apply the ruling to the issues in question.

(4) The ToA amended the EC Treaty to give the ECJ power to consider preliminary references in two new areas. Under Art.68, EC national courts, against whose decisions there is no judicial remedy, must refer to the ECJ questions concerning measures under Title IV (relating to visas, asylum, immigration, etc.). The wording of Art.68 precludes references from the lower courts: *Dem Yanenko* (Case C-45/03). The Council, Commission and Member States have discretion to refer in such circumstances. Under Title VI, where the Member States accept the jurisdiction of the ECJ (Art.35 TEU), the ECJ may make preliminary rulings in relation to framework decisions (harmonisation measures under the third pillar). (See Chapter One) For a ruling on a framework decision, see *Maria Pupina* (Case C-105/03) (see Ch.1, p.14).

(5) The CFI was given the power to hear questions referred for a preliminary ruling under Art.234 by the TN in specific areas laid down by the Statute of the Court. Where the CFI consider that the case requires a decision of principle likely to affect the unity or consistency of EC law, it may refer the case to the ECJ for hearing. Decisions of the CFI under Art.234 may (exceptionally) be reviewed by the ECJ under conditions and limits laid down by the Statute where there is a serious risk of the unity or consistency of EC law being affected.

Discretionary References

Court or tribunal

Key Principle: **Any court or tribunal of a Member State has the power to make a reference under Art.234 to the ECJ.**

Broekmeulen v Huisarts Registratie Commissie (Case 246/80) 1981
A Dutch Appeals Committee for General Medicine (not regarded as a court or tribunal under Dutch law) refused B's application to practice as a doctor in the Netherlands. During the course of a reference the ECJ considered whether the Committee was a court or tribunal for the purpose of Art.234 (ex 177).

Held: (ECJ) Where there is no right of appeal to the ordinary courts, the Appeals Committee, which operates with the consent of the public authorities and with their co-operation and which delivers decisions which are final after an adversarial procedure, must be regarded as a court or tribunal for the purpose of Art.234 (ex 177). [1981] E.C.R. 2311.

Commentary

(1) For a body to be considered a court or tribunal under Art.234 it is essential that the body in question exercises a judicial function (by making legally binding decisions), is competent to make a reference and is subject to control by public authorities. These elements were found by the ECJ to be lacking in *Nordsee Deutsch Hochseefischerei GmbH* (Case 102/81) where an arbitrator was appointed without participation of public authorities, under a contract in which recourse to arbitration was voluntary.

(2) A body exercising a purely administrative function is not covered by Art.234. See, for example, *Victoria Film* (Case C-134/97) (body acting in administrative capacity making binding decisions on matters of individual tax planning).

(3) Where a body exercises both judicial and administrative functions, it will not be treated as a court or tribunal for the purpose of Art.234 when exercising an administrative function: *Radiotelevisione Italiana* (RAI) (Case C-440/98), in this case a retrospective review by the Corte dei Conte involving

the assessing and checking of the results of administrative activity was considered by the ECJ to be an administrative function.

(4) The characteristics required of a court or tribunal were listed in *Dorsch Consult* (Case C-54/96) as including whether the body is established by law, its jurisdiction is compulsory, its procedure adversarial, whether it applies rules of law and whether it is independent. The last factor, "independence", was the subject of a ruling in joined Cases C-110/98 *Gabalfrisa* and C-147/98 *Abrahamson*. In *Gabalfrisa* the ECJ found that there was a separation of functions between the tax authorities and a Spanish tax tribunal which heard complaints against the decisions of those authorities within the framework of internal administrative action. In *Abrahamson* an appeals committee with independent power to examine appeals against appointments in universities in Sweden was found to have the character of a third party and to be functionally separate. In both cases, the bodies were found to be courts or tribunals under Art.234.

Necessity

Key Principle: **Where a question of interpretation or validity of EC law is raised before a court or tribunal of a Member State, that court or tribunal may, if it considers that a question is necessary to enable it to give judgment, request the ECJ to give a ruling on it (Art.234(2)).**

CILFIT Srl. and Lanificio di Gavardo Spa. v Ministry of Health (Case 283/81) 1982
Wool importers disputed a health inspection levy imposed by the Italian Government on wool imported from outside the EC, arguing that wool is an animal product (for which charges could not be imposed by regulation) and therefore not subject to such a charge. The Italian Government claimed that the interpretation of "animal product" was obvious under the acte clair principle, in which case no reference under Art.234 (ex 177) was necessary. The Italian Supreme Court referred the question to the ECJ.

Held: (ECJ) A reference to the ECJ is not necessary where:

(1) the question of EC law is irrelevant;

(2) the question has already been decided by the ECJ; and

(3) the correct interpretation is so obvious as to leave no scope for doubt. [1982] E.C.R. 3415.

Commentary

(1) While the ruling in *CILFIT* was formulated in response to a question concerning mandatory references under Art.234 (ex 177(3)) (see below), it applies also to discretionary references. The "*acte clair*" doctrine derives from French administrative law: international treaties need not be referred to the government for interpretation if the meaning is clear. The ECJ in 1996 issued Notes for Guidance to National Courts for Preliminary Rulings, to provide a summary of advice from the caselaw of the Court on making a reference, reaffirming its position on decisions such as *CILFIT*.

(2) In *Bulmer v Bollinger* (CA, 1974) [1974] 2 All E.R. 1226, Lord Denning drew up guidelines for the United Kingdom courts in making Art.177 (now 234) references. The guidelines, though not binding, were treated as influential. Factors to be taken into account were stated to include the existence of a previous ECJ ruling, the conclusiveness of the reference to the judgment, the need to establish the facts, delay, the wishes of the parties and costs. Lord Denning's guidelines have been criticised as unduly restrictive. They should not be followed where they conflict with *CILFIT*.

(3) The Court of Appeal ruled that three factors must be present if a reference is to be made: the facts must be clear, the provision of EC law must be conclusive to the determination of the case and the judge must consider whether he himself can resolve the question of EC law with complete confidence (*R. v International Stock Exchange of the UK and the Republic of Ireland, Ex p. Else* [1993] 1 All E.R. 420.

Mandatory references

Key Principle: **Where a question of interpretation or validity of EC Law is raised before any court or tribunal of a Member State against whose decisions there is no judicial remedy, that**

court or tribunal shall bring the matter before the ECJ (Art.234(3)).

Costa v ENEL (Case 6/64) 1964

Several questions were referred to the ECJ by the Italian small claims court (see Ch.1, p.4). As the sum claimed was very low there was no right of appeal to a higher national court.

Held: (ECJ) National courts against whose decisions there is no judicial remedy must refer the matter to the ECJ. [1964] E.C.R. 585.

Commentary

(1) Identification of the courts that are covered by the obligation to refer under Art.234(3) has been controversial. United Kingdom courts have been reluctant to accept that courts other than the House of Lords are obliged to refer. The position of the Court of Appeal and other lower courts has been difficult to determine. It may be impossible to know until a case is concluded whether the Court of Appeal is the court of last resort or not (i.e. whether leave to appeal against a decision of the CA will be granted by the CA itself or by the HL). The ECJ has not ruled on this point. The present uncertainties are illustrated by *S.A. Magnavision N.V. v General Optical Council.* The High Court had refused leave to appeal to the House of Lords against conviction on a point of EC law (*Magnavision No.1* (QBD, 1987)). The Divisional Court in *Magnavision No.2* (QBD, 1987) refused leave to appeal on a point of public importance (whether the Divisional Court became a court of final resort when leave to appeal to the HL was refused), ruling that the matter was closed. The applicant was left without a remedy. While no clear precedent exists in English law the United Kingdom courts appear to be moving towards acceptance of the wide view as expressed in *Costa v ENEL* rather than the narrow view in *Magnavision*.

(2) *Kobler v Austria* (Case C-224/01) (See Ch.1, p. 20) has been seen by Szyszczak and Cygan in *Understanding EU Law* (Sweet & Maxwell, 2005) at p.50 as reinforcing a literal interpretation of the duty to refer under Art.234(3). "In this judgment the Court appears to reject the view that *acte clair* can be applied by courts of last instance and takes a pragmatic view of Art.234."

(3) Where an appeal lies from national court or tribunal to the national supreme court only if that supreme court declares that the appeal is admissible is *not* regarded as a court of last resort under Art.234(3), and so is not under an obligation to refer: *Lyckeskog* (Case C-99/00).

Key Principle: **References under Art.234 are not precluded by the existence of a prior ruling of the ECJ on a similar point.**

Da Costa en Schake N.V. v Nederlandse Belastagingenad-ministratie (Cases 28-30/62) 1963
A Dutch court of last resort referred questions identical to those in *Van Gend en Loos* (see Ch.1, p.3) on which judgment had recently been given by the ECJ. The Commission argued that the reference should be dismissed for lack of cause, as no questions remained for interpretation.

Held: (ECJ) Where an authoritative ruling has been made on an identical point, a national court need not refer. However, no national court may be deprived of the opportunity to refer a provision that has already been interpreted. [1963] E.C.R. 31.

Commentary

(1) The ECJ does not operate a formal doctrine of binding precedent. Nevertheless, it does tend in most cases to follow its own previous decisions. In *Da Costa* the Court stated that making a reference on a point materially identical to a previous ruling may "deprive the obligation [to refer under Art.234 (ex 177(3))] of its purpose and thus empty it of its substance". The national court was directed to the judgment in *Van Gend en Loos*. Where the ECJ intends to depart from its own previous decision it normally makes the change of direction very clear. (See, e.g. *Keck* and *Mithouard* (Joined Cases C-267 & 268/91) (Ch.8, p.91).

(2) Where a question referred to the ECJ is manifestly identical to a question on which the Court has ruled earlier, it may, under Art.104 of its Rules of Procedure, give its decision by reasoned order in which reference is made to the previous judgment. This rule was invoked for the first time in relation to interpretation in *Beton Express v Direction Regionale des*

Douanes de la Reunion (Cases C-405(408/96) and in relation to validity in *Conata and Agrindustria v Aimaa* (Cases C-332 & 333/96).

Misuse of the Article 234 Procedure

Key Principle: **Questions referred by national courts must involve genuine issues of EC law or they will not be considered by the ECJ.**

Foglia v Novella (No.1) (Case 104/79) (1980)
F and N, wine dealers in France and Italy, inserted a clause in their contract of sale not to pay any tax that contravened EC law. F sought to recover from N the tax incurred by a carrier of the goods in France. It appeared that the parties might have artificially concocted the contractual terms and the litigation in order to obtain a ruling on the validity of the French law.

Held: (ECJ) It is the duty of the ECJ to supply rulings in genuine disputes. To rule in circumstances such as the present case would jeopardise the system by which individuals can protect themselves against tax provisions contrary to the Treaty. [1980] E.C.R. 745.

Commentary

(1) The ECJ refused to rule in *Foglia v Novella* (No.1) and remitted the case to the national court. Undeterred, the Italian court made a further attempt to refer the same questions to the ECJ in *Foglia v Novella* (No.2) (Case 244/80). Again the ECJ refused to answer, stating that the Court must be especially vigilant when asked to consider the validity of the national laws of another Member State. The decision has been criticised as unhelpful to the national court faced with a real, not a hypothetical problem (the validity of the tax under EC law). See also *Meilicke* (Case C-83/91) (refusal to rule on academic issue regarded by the ECJ as an artificial question).

(2) The ECJ has declined to rule in a number of cases. See, e.g. *SPUC v Grogan* (Case C-159/90) in which no ruling was made in relation to public policy and the availability of information about abortion services because the information was available without charge and so was outside the scope of Art.59 (now 49).

(3) Compare with *Dzodzi v Belgium* (Joined Cases C-297/88 & 197/89) (application of EC social security rules outside the EC where national law made reference to EC rules). The ECJ was prepared to make a ruling in order to ensure the uniform application of EC law.

(4) *Andersson v Sweden* (Case C-321/97) concerned a question of interpretation of the EEA Agreement (an agreement between various EFTA states and the EU). As the agreement involved the application of the agreement in the EFTA states and arose prior to Sweden's accession to the EU, the ECJ ruled that it had no jurisdiction to consider the question.

Rulings on validity

Key Principle: **While national courts may declare that a provision of EC law is valid, only the ECJ may declare a provision of EC law invalid.**

Foto-Frost v Hauptzollamt Lubeck-Ost (Case 314/85) 1987

A German court referred to the ECJ the question of whether a national court could declare invalid a provision of EC law (in this case, a decision which appeared to conflict with a regulation).

Held: (ECJ) National courts have no jurisdiction to declare that acts of EC institutions are invalid. [1987] E.C.R. 4199.

Commentary
In Foto-Frost the ECJ stated that an exception to the rule might arise in the event of an applicant seeking an interim injunction (although no question had been referred on this point). The issue was taken up in *Zuckerfabrik* (see below).

Key Principle: **The national courts are not precluded by Art.249 (ex 189) of the Treaty from suspending enforcement of a national administrative measure adopted on the basis of an EC regulation.**

Zuckerfabrik Suderdithmarschen A.G. v Hauptzollamt Itzehoe (Case C-143/88) 1991

Z, a sugar producer, complained that a German decision imposing a levy based on an EC regulation was invalid. The German court referred a number of questions to the ECJ, including the possible basis for the suspension of a national measure based on a regulation that may be invalid.

Held: (ECJ) A national court may suspend a national measure adopted to implement an EC regulation if:

(1) the national court entertains serious doubts as to the validity of the EC measure and itself refers the question of validity to the ECJ (if this has not already been done);

(2) there is urgency and a threat of serious and irreparable damage to the applicant;

(3) the national court takes due account of the EC's interests. [1991] E.C.R. I-415.

Commentary

(1) Due to the time needed to obtain an Art.234 (ex 177) reference from the ECJ (up to two years) the need for an interim remedy pending final resolution of the issues has become great in a number of cases. In *R. v Secretary of State for Transport, Ex p. Factortame the House of Lords* applied the ruling of the ECJ in Case 213/89 (see Ch.1) and suspended the offending parts of the Merchant Shipping Act 1988. The House of Lords held that interim relief was necessary to protect the rights of individuals under EC law.

(2) The ECJ introduced a simplified procedure in 2000. This may be involved in three circumstances:

- Where the question referred is identical to one referred earlier:
- Where the answer to the question may clearly be deduced from existing caselaw: or
- Where the answer to the question admits of no reasonable doubt.

Using the procedure enables the ECJ to provide a response within five months rather than the usual 24.

8. FREE MOVEMENT OF GOODS

The Customs Union

Key Principle: **Member States are required under Art.23 (ex 9) EC to form a customs union. They must not introduce any new customs duties between Member States, nor must they increase existing duties (Art.25 (ex 12)).**

Van Gend en Loos v Nederlandse Administratie der Belastingen (Case 26/62) 1963
For facts, see Ch.1, p.4.

Held: (ECJ) Art.12 (now 25) is directly effective. [1963] E.C.R. 1.

Commentary
The customs union involves the prohibition between Member States of customs duties on imports and exports and of charges having equivalent effect, and the adoption of a customs tariff in relation to third countries (non-Member States) (Art.25 (ex 12)).

Van Gend en Loos illustrates the importance attached by the ECJ to the customs union by recognising that individuals may enforce their rights under Art.25 (ex 12) before the national courts.

Key Principle: **A charge having equivalent effect which is disguised as a tax or levy is illegal under Art.25 (ex 12).**

Sociaal Fonds voor de Diamantarbeiders v S.A.C. Brachfeld (Cases 2 & 3/69) 1969
The Belgian Government imposed a levy on imported diamonds in order to provide social security benefits for diamond workers. An Art.234 (ex 177) reference was made to the ECJ.

Held: (ECJ) The imposition of a charge on goods crossing a frontier is an obstacle to the free movement of goods. Such a levy is prohibited under Art.12 independently of its destination or purpose. [1969] E.C.R. 211.

Commentary
If the diamond workers' welfare scheme had been funded through a non-discriminatory system of taxation without reference to imports it would have been permissible under Art.90 (ex 95) (see below).

Discriminatory Taxation

Key Principle: **No Member State may impose a tax directly or indirectly on products from another Member State greater than that applied to similar domestic products. Indirect protection through taxation of domestic products is also illegal: Art.90 (ex 95).**

Commission v UK (Re Excise Duties on Wine) (No.1) (Case 170/78) 1980
The Commission sought a declaration under Art.226 (ex 169) that the United Kingdom had infringed Art.90 (ex 95) by imposing a higher excise duty on light wines than on beers.

Held: (ECJ) Allowing for changing drinking habits and the increasing popularity of wine in the United Kingdom it is possible to regard wine and beer as similar products in competition with each other and to compare the taxation of each. No ruling was made pending further investigation. [1980] E.C.R. 417.

Held: (No.2) (Case 170/78A) 1983: (ECJ) (Following the investigation by the Commission) The United Kingdom tax system discriminated against imported wine so as to afford a protection to domestically produced beer, contrary to Art.95. [1983] E.C.R. 2265.

Commentary

(1) Art.86 (ex 90) allows Member States freedom to create their own internal systems of taxation provided there is no discrimination between Member States. Similar products may be taxed differently only where the distinction is objectively justified. In *Commission v France* (Case 196/85) there was no breach when traditional sweet wines were taxed at a lower rate than ordinary wines to provide economic assistance to rural areas dependent on wine production.

(2) In *Humblot v Directeur des Services Fiscaux* (Case 112/84) road tax was payable to the French Government at a higher rate on cars of more than 16 c-v, the highest engine capacity for cars made in France. A French taxpayer sought to recover the additional tax paid on a 36 c-v car imported from Germany. The ECJ held the system to be a breach of Art.90 (ex 95). An amended tax system was later found still to breach Art.90 (ex 95).

Quantitative Restrictions and Measures having Equivalent Effect

Key Principle: **Quantitative restrictions and all measures having equivalent effect are prohibited under Art.28 (ex 30).**

R. v Henn and Darby (Case 34/79) 1980
The United Kingdom seized pornographic goods imported from the Netherlands. The importers were prosecuted and an Art.234 (ex 177) reference was made by the House of Lords.

Held: (ECJ) A total ban is a quantitative restriction under Art.28 (ex 30). (The measure was in fact found to be justified under Art.30 (ex 36): see p.84.) [1979] E.C.R. 3795.

Commentary

(1) Anything which restricts importation by reference to quantity (e.g. a quota system) is a quantitative restriction.

(2) The Treaty renumbering resulting from the ToA has had aparticularly unfortunate effect in relation to the provisions on the free movement of goods as old Art.30 has become Art.28 and old Art.36, new Art.30 (with old Arts 31—33 repealed). It is thus essential to be sure, in relation to any citation of "Art.30", whether this relates to new or old numbering.

(3) Inactions as well as actions may be a breach of Art.28. In *Commission v France* (Case C-265/95) the Commission brought enforcement proceedings against France under Art.226 (ex 169) for failing to act to prevent disruption to the free movement of agricultural goods such as Spanish strawberries. The problems arose from protest action by French farmers and others, intercepting lorries, destroying

their loads and threatening their drivers. The ECJ held that the French Government's failure to adopt necessary and proportionate measures was a breach of Art.10 (ex 5) EC.

Key Principle: **All trading rules enacted by Member States which are capable of hindering, directly or indirectly, actually or potentially, intra-EC trade are to be considered as measures having an effect equivalent to quantitative restrictions.**

Procureur du Roi v Dassonville (Case 8/74) 1974
Dassonville, a trader, imported Scotch whisky into Belgium from France without a certificate of origin, contrary to Belgian law. He was charged with a criminal offence but pleaded that the Belgian requirement contravened Art.28 (ex 30). An Art.234 (ex 177) reference was made.

Held: (ECJ) In the absence of harmonisation, a Member State may take measures to prevent unfair practices provided they are reasonable and do not hinder inter-member trade. It was more difficult for a trader importing goods in circulation in another Member State to obtain a certificate than for an importer to do so when importing the goods directly from the state of production. Thus the requirement to obtain a certificate was a measure having equivalent effect and was illegal under Art.28 (ex 30). [1974] E.C.R. 837.

Commentary

(1) *Dassonville* is important in that it defines what is meant by a "measure having equivalent effect" (MEQR). Further examples of MEQRs include inspection fees at frontiers and charges for storage pending inspections. Following the decision in *Keck and Mithouard* (see p.91) a more restrictive approach has been taken by the ECJ to measures regarded as MEQRs.

(2) Directive 70/50 divides measures into distinctly effectivemeasures (which do not apply equally to domestic and imported goods) and indistinctly effective measures (which apply alike to both domestic and imported goods).

(3) Under Art.3 of Directive 70/50 indistinctly appli-
cablemeasures only infringe Art.28 (ex 30) when they are
disproportionate, i.e. more restrictive than necessary to
achieve their objective.

Key Principle: **Member States may not promote national
products where this involves discrimination against imports.**

Commission v Ireland (Case 249/81) 1982
A scheme was operated ("Buy Irish") to promote the sales of
Irish goods to shoppers in Ireland. A symbol indicating Irish
origin was attached to goods and an information service was
available. According to the Irish Government the scheme was
not particularly successful as the sale of imported products
actually rose during the promotion period. The Commission
brought an action against the Irish Government under Art.226
(ex 169).

Held: (ECJ) If a measure is capable of restricting imports it is
illegal under Art.28 (ex 30). [1982] E.C.R. 4005.

Commentary
Contrast the "Buy Irish" case with *Apple and Pear Council v Lewis*
(Case 222/82) in which a Council funded by a levy on apple and
pear growers in England and Wales was created to promote the
consumption of English and Welsh varieties. Some growers refused
to pay, claiming that the scheme infringed Art.28 (ex 30). The ECJ
(under Art.234 (ex 177)) held that it was permissible to promote a
product by reference to its qualities, even where those qualities are
typical of national production.

Key Principle: **There is no valid reason why goods which
have been lawfully produced and marketed in one Member
State should not be introduced into any other Member State
(the principle of mutual recognition).**

Rewe-Zentral A.G. v Bundesmonopolverwaltung fur Brannt-
wein ("Cassis de Dijon") (Case 120/78 1979)
Cassis de Dijon is a blackcurrant liqueur originating in France
where it contains 15 to 20 per cent alcohol by volume. German

law required fruit liqueurs to have a minimum alcohol content of 25 per cent. While the measure was not discriminatory it clearly excluded French cassis from the German market. German importers challenged the measure in the national court which made an Art.234 (ex 177) reference.

Held: In the absence of EC rules, the Member States may regulate the production and marketing of alcoholic drinks. Obstacles to movement within the EC arising from disparities between national laws relating to the marketing of the products must be accepted in so far as they may be necessary to satisfy mandatory requirements relating in particular to the effectiveness of fiscal supervision, the protection of public health, fairness of commercial transactions and the defence of the consumer. [1979] E.C.R. 649.

Commentary

(1) The ECJ rejected German Government claims that a requirement for a higher alcohol content discouraged alcoholism and that it protected consumers against unfair commercial practices. The requirement infringed the principle of proportionality and, while mandatory, was not necessary. Consumers could be protected by being given information about the alcoholic content on the label.

(2) The mandatory requirements in *Cassis* have provided a basis for departing from Art.28 (ex 30) in cases involving indistinctly applicable measures. They were not satisfied in *Commission v Germany* (Case 178/84) in which a long-standing ban on additives in beer was found to be unjustifiable on health grounds. Other unjustifiable measures have included a restriction on the shape of bottles containing traditional alcoholic drinks and a requirement to sell margarine in cubes.

(3) Note that distinctly applicable measures may only be justified under Art.30 (ex 36) (see p.94).

(4) The principle of mutual recognition represents a widening of the *Cassis* principle to cover all goods, not merely alcoholic beverages. It has provided the basis for the single market (1992) programme of directives to harmonise standards.

Key Principle: **National strategies to protect the environment may infringe Art.28 (ex 30).**

Commission v Denmark (Case 302/86) 1988

Danish law required that beer and soft drinks could be sold only in reusable containers, as part of a deposit-and-return scheme on grounds of environmental protection. The scheme was later modified to allow producers to market a limited quantity of drinks in non-approved containers. The Commission brought an action under Art.226 (ex 169) in the ECJ, claiming that the measure infringed Art.28 (ex 30).

Held: (ECJ) Although protection of the environment is an important objective, the quantitative restriction on beverages that could be sold in non-approved containers had a disproportionate effect on importers from other EC states. Denmark was in breach of Art.28 (ex 30). [1988] E.C.R. 4607.

Commentary

(1) This case illustrates the difficult position of a Member State introducing a measure that can affect imports, in the absence of common EC rules. Contrast the decision with *Oebel* (Case 155/80) in which a Belgian law forbidding night working in bakeries was held not to infringe Art.28 (ex 30) because it did not affect imports.

(2) In another case concerned with the environmental problems associated with drinks packaging, this time where common EC rules have been adopted, the court found that problems can still occur where harmonisation is not complete. *Commission v Germany* (Case C-463/01) concerned enforcement proceedings brought against Germany which required the producers and distributors of drinks in non-reusable packaging to charge a deposit and take back the packaging. As Directive 94/62 on packaging and packaging waste (requiring producers of mineral water to bottle at source) did not fully harmonise the law, the German legislation had to be assessed for compatibility Art.28. While the German rules could be justified as necessary to protect the environment, they infringed the principle of proportionality as the transition period for producers and distributors to adopt was only six months.

Key Principle: **The regulation of Sunday trading falls within the discretion of Member States to make political and economic choices to accord with national or regional sociocultural characteristics.**

Torfaen Borough Council v B&Q Plc (Case 145/88) 1989
The defendant was charged with trading on a Sunday contrary to the Shops Act 1950. The magistrates court referred to the ECJ the question of whether such a measure breached Art.28 (ex 30).

Held: (ECJ) It is a legitimate part of socio-economic policy for Member States to regulate opening hours. Such rules do not infringe Art.28 (ex 30) provided they are not disproportionate and do not affect inter-member trade. [1989] E.C.R. 3851.

Commentary

(1) *Torfaen* left many shops and local authorities in confusion over Sunday trading. Later decisions clarified the position. The ECJ stated unequivocally in *Stoke on Trent and Norwich City Council v B&Q* (Cases C-169/91) that the prohibition in Art.28 (ex 30) does not apply to national legislation prohibiting retailers from opening their premises on Sundays. The Sunday trading laws did not discriminate against imports. Their legitimacy turned on proportionality (weighing national interests in achieving the objective against EC interests in the free movement of goods).

(2) A ban on the employment of labour in France and Belgium on Sundays was also outside Art.28 (ex 30): *Marchandise* (Case C-332/89) and *Conforama* (Case C-312/89).

(3) The Sunday Trading Act 1994 now permits shops in England and Wales below a certain floor area to trade freely on Sundays. Larger shops may trade for six hours between 10am and 6pm.

Key Principle: **Art.28 (ex 30) does not apply to selling arrangements by Member States which do not affect inter-member trade.**

Keck and Mithouard (Joined Cases C-267 & 268/91) 1993
K and M had resold goods at a loss contrary to French law. They claimed that the prohibition restricted the volume of sales

of imported goods and so infringed Art.28 (ex 30). An Art.234 (ex 177) reference was made.

Held: (ECJ) Contrary to what had previously been decided, the application to products from other Member States of national provisions restricting or partitioning certain selling arrangements does not hinder directly or indirectly, actually or potentially, trade between Member States within the meaning of the *Dassonville* judgment. [1993] E.C.R. I-6097.

Commentary

(1) *Keck and Mithouard* signals a departure from the previous line of case law developed by the ECJ since Cassis. Traders had relied too heavily on Art.28 (ex 30) to challenge national measures restricting commercial freedom where there was no effect on imports. Member States should be free to adopt measures that do not affect inter-member trade, provided these conform to the principle of proportionality.

(2) Later cases have confirmed this approach. In *Tankstation't Heukste vof and Boermans* (Case C-401/92) Dutch rules on opening hours of shops in petrol stations were held to be outside Art.28 (ex 30). A similar finding was made in *Hunermund v* Landesapothekerkammer Baden-Wurttemberg (Case C-292/92) (prohibition on promotion of para-pharmaceutical products outside pharmacies). See also *Belgapom v Itm Belgium and Vocarex S.A.* (Case C-63/94). (Potatoes were sold at a loss contrary to Belgian law. Held: (ECJ) Art.28 (ex 30) does not apply to national legislation prohibiting sales at a very low profit margin.) For other instances of selling arrangements being left to the discretion of national authorities, see *Societe d'Importation Edouard Leclerc-Siplec v TFI Publicité S.A. and M6 Publicité S.A.* (Case C-412/93) (a French ban on televised advertising of the distribution sector) and *Konsumentombudsmannen (KO) v Gourmet International Products AB (GIP)* (Case C-405/98) (Swedish legislation prohibiting the advertising of alcoholic drinks justified in the interests of public health).

(3) In some cases, by contrast, the ECJ has found that nationalselling arrangements place a dual burden of regulation, with control exercised both at the state of production and the state of sale. In such circumstances the measure

is in breach of Art.28. See *Verband SozialerWettbewerb eV v Clinique Labaratoires SNCF* (Case C-315/92). The effect of a German law banning the use of the name "Clinique" for cosmetics was to require the repackaging of imported cosmetics to be sold in Germany. As the ECJ did not accept that the ban was justified to avoid confusing customers, the measure infringed Art.28. Similar reasoning was employed in another case of German origin, this time involving national restrictions on unfair competition: *Verein gegen Unwesen in Handel und Gewerbe Köln v Mars GmbH* (Case C-470/93) (Requirement to repackage Mars bars with the words "plus ten percent" on the wrapping for sale in Germany infringed Art.29 (ex 30)). In *Georg Schwarz v Bürgermeister der Landeshaupstadt Salzburg* (Case C-366/04) the ECJ found that a ban by Austria on the sale of unwrapped chewing gum from automatic vending machines imposed an additional burden on importers, the ban was justified on grounds of public health.

Key Principle: **Each case should be assessed on its merits to determine the actual or potential effect of national legislation in relation to Art.28 (ex 30).**

Neeltje v Houtwipper (Case C-293/93) 1994
Dutch law required all precious metals to be hallmarked according to certain specifications before being offered for sale. Thus imported goods would require re-hallmarking on entering the Netherlands. An Art.234 (ex 177) reference was made.

Held: (ECJ) While the hallmarking requirement was a mandatory measure to protect consumers and promote fair-trading, it infringed Art.28 (ex 30) by requiring the fixing of a fresh hallmark where an equivalent hallmark had already been affixed in another Member State. [1994] E.C.R. I-4249.

Commentary
Unlike *Keck and Mithouard* the measure in *Neeltje* discriminated against imports.

Quantitative restrictions on exports and measures having equivalent effect

Key Principle: **Restrictions on exports will only breach Art.29 (ex 34) if they have as their object or effect the restriction of patterns of exports, providing an advantage to the home product or market.**

Groenveld v Produktschap voor Vee en Vlees (Case 15/79) 1979

Dutch law prohibited all meat processors from stocking or processing horsemeat, in order to prevent the export of horse-meat to countries prohibiting its sale. Groenveld decided to make horsemeat sausages, contrary to Dutch law, claiming that the law infringed Art.29 (ex 34) by prohibiting the processing and exporting of horsemeat.

Held: (ECJ) Art.29 (ex 34) did not apply to a rule which did not discriminate between goods for the home market and for export. [1989] E.C.R. 3967

Commentary

(1) The *Cassis* justifications for restrictions on imports do not apply to exports. Whereas importers face a "dual burden", namely the requirements of the home state and of the importing state, exporters need only satisfy the requirements of the home state. Thus export restrictions may only be justified under Art.30 (ex 36).

(2) "Quantitative restrictions" and "measures having equivalent effect" have the same meanings for Art.29 (ex 34) as for Art.28 (ex 30).

Derogations from Articles 30 to 34 (ex 28 and 29)

Key Principle: **Arts 30 to 34 (ex 28 and 29) do not preclude prohibitions on imports, exports or goods in transit justified on grounds of public morality, public policy or public security; the protection of life or health of humans, animals or plants; the protection of national treasures possessing artistic, historic or archaeological value; or the protection of industrial** or commercial property. Such prohibitions must not constitute a means of arbitrary discrimination or a disguised restriction on trade between Member States: Art.30 (ex 36).

Key Principle: Restrictions on imports or exports may be justified on grounds of public morality.

R. v Henn and Darby (Case 34/79) 1979

See p.86. The United Kingdom seized films and publications being imported from the Netherlands into the United Kingdom. The importers were prosecuted under customs and excise legislation with importing indecent and obscene arts. In their defence the importers claimed that the prohibition contravened Art.28 (ex 30) in that a stricter standard was being applied to imported than to domestic goods. An Art.234 (ex 177) reference was made.

Held: (ECJ) A Member State may lawfully prohibit on grounds of public morality the importation from another Member State of indecent or obscene materials as understood by its domestic laws. A prohibition on imports that is stricter than the domestic prohibition is not a measure designed to give indirect protection to a national product or aimed at creating arbitrary discrimination depending on where the goods are produced. [1979] E.C.R. 3795.

Commentary

Henn and Darby illustrates the general requirement of Art.30 (ex 36) that a measure must be necessary, but must not involve arbitrary discrimination or a disguised restriction on inter-member trade. Contrast *Conegate Ltd v HM Customs and Excise* (Case 121/85) in which there was a lawful domestic trade in the goods in question (inflatable dolls). Seizure of dolls being imported from Germany into the United Kingdom on grounds that they were indecent and obscene was a breach of Art.28 (ex 30), being discriminatory on grounds of nationality.

Key Principle: Restrictions on imports or exports may be justified on grounds of public policy.

R. v Thompson (Case 7/78) 1978

United Kingdom law in force at the time prohibited the importation of gold coins and export of silver-alloy coins minted before 1947. The case turned on the distinction between whether the coins were "goods" or "means of payment". Under United Kingdom law it was illegal to melt down or destroy coins, even if they were no longer legal tender.

Held: (ECJ) As the coins were not legal tender they were goods under Art.28 (ex 30). A ban on destroying such coins with a view to preventing their being melted down or destroyed in another Member State was justified on grounds of public policy under Art.30 (ex 36), because it stemmed from the need to protect the right to mint coinage which is traditionally regarded as involving the fundamental interests of the state. [1978] E.C.R. 2247.

Commentary

(1) "Public policy" is a translation of the French term "ordrepublic". *R. v Thompson* is a rare example of a successful invocation of the exception. Public policy does not cover consumer protection (*Kohl v Ringelhan* (Case 177/83)) or economic considerations (*Cullet v Centre Leclerc* (Case 213/83)).

(2) For a House of Lords ruling on public policy under Art.30 (ex 36) in the context of a restriction on exports, see *R. v Chief Constable of Sussex, Ex p. Trader's Ferry* [1998] 2 W.L.R. 1260. This case concerned a decision by the Chief Constable of Sussex to reduce the level of policing at the port of Shoreham where there had been a prolonged campaign of protest against the export of live animals to the continent. (The Chief Constable had justified his decision on the basis that policing the prolonged campaign reduced his capacity to carry out other policing responsibilities.) International Trader's Ferry, the exporter, sought judicial review of the Chief Constable's decision. The HL held that the Chief Constable had not acted unreasonably in English law. Without making a reference to the ECJ, the HL held that, assuming the decision to be a measure equivalent to a quantitative restriction on exports under Art.29 (ex 34), it was justified on grounds of public policy. Such grounds could arise where the broader requirements of public policy

justified steps being taken. The Chief Constable's actions were proportionate and reasonable in the light of available resources.

Key Principle: **Restrictions on imports or exports may be justified by public security.**

Campus Oil v Minister for Industry and Energy (Case 72/83) 1984
Irish law required importers of petroleum products to buy up to 35 per cent of their needs from the Irish National Petroleum Company (INPC) at fixed prices. Ireland sought to justify this requirement on both public policy and public security grounds, claiming that this was the only method by which the national refining capacity could be maintained and the products sold.

Held: (ECJ) The measure was justified on grounds of public security rather than public policy. Maintaining a refinery enabled Ireland to enter into long-term contracts with oil producers who would ensure greater continuity of oil supplies during a crisis. [1983] E.C.R. 2727.

Commentary
The ECJ accepted that a measure justified on grounds of public security might also achieve economic objectives without taking it outside Art.30 (ex 36).

Key Principle: **Restrictions on imports and exports may be justified on grounds of protection of life and health of humans, animals or plants.**

Officier van Justitie v Kaasfabrik Eyssen B.V. (Case 53/80) 1981
A cheese producer was prosecuted in the Netherlands for using nisin, a preservative prohibited under Dutch law, in processed cheese. Nisin was a permitted ingredient in other Member States. Scientific research was divided as to the harmfulness of the additive. The cheese producer argued that the ban infringed Art.28 (ex 30) as it impeded imports.

Held: (ECJ) In the absence of harmonisation, a state may protect the public by banning additives where there is genuine scientific doubt about their safety. [1981] E.C.R. 409.

Commentary

(1) This decision forms part of a series of cases on the use of additives (cf. *Commission v Germany*, see p.89). In *Ministre Public v Claude Muller* (Case 304/84) it was held that the requirement for authorisation for specific additives is subject to the principle of proportionality; thus the process of application must be rapid and straightforward. Prior national authorisation may also be required for medical products (*Lucien Ortscheit GmbH v Eurim-Pharm GmbH* (Case C-320/93).

(2) Note that the protection of public health is a consideration that outweighs all others, especially economic considerations: *Boehringer v Council* (Joined Cases T-125 &126/96).

Key Principle: **The risk to health must be real and form part of a seriously considered health policy.**

Commission v UK (Case 40/82) 1982

The United Kingdom unilaterally and hastily introduced a ban on the importation of poultry meat and eggs after extensive lobbying by United Kingdom poultry producers just before Christmas 1981. The United Kingdom Government claimed that the measure was necessary under Art.30 (ex 36) to prevent British flocks catching a form of poultry disease known as Newcastle Disease. Enforcement proceedings were brought against the UK.

Held: (ECJ) The ban was not part of a health policy but was a disguised restriction on trade. Less restrictive methods would have been sufficient. The measure could not be justified on grounds of animal health under Art.30 (ex 36). [1982] E.C.R. 2793.

Commentary

The measure appeared to be an attempt to protect United Kingdom producers from French competition. French turkey farmers later sought to recover their losses from the United Kingdom Government in *Burgoin v MAFF* (CA). Although the claim was struck out they won an out of court settlement of £3.5 million.

Key Principle: **Where there is uncertainty as to the existence or extent of risks to human health, the institutions may take protective measures without having to wait until the illegality and seriousness of those risks becomes fully apparent.**

National Farmers' Union and Others (Case C-157/96); United Kingdom v Commission (Case C-180/96)
The Commission adopted emergency measures in 1996 to counteract the threat to health posed by B.S.E. ("mad cow disease") prohibiting the UK from exporting beef worldwide. The UK contested the decision under Art.230 (ex 173). The ECJ considered that the Commission was entitled to react to the publication of new information about the disease, and that the confinement of animals and products within a particular territory was an appropriate measure, even in relation to exports to third countries.

Held: (ECJ) (1) The measures were not disproportionate: there was no need to wait until the full extent of the risks became apparent.

(2) The measures were not illegal, and were properly based on Art.37 (ex 43) on the Common Agricultural Policy. [1998] E.C.R. I-2211; [1998] E.C.R. I-2265.

Commentary

(1) In *Commission v France* (Case C-1/00) the Commission brought enforcement proceedings against France for unilaterally maintaining the export ban on British beef after the ban was lifted in August 1999 for certain meats and meat products. While declaring that France had acted unlawfully in refusing to adopt the necessary measure to implement the lifting of the ban, the ECJ found that its failure was not as extensive as the Commission had claimed, in view (partly) of the difficulty in interpreting and implementing the relevant Commission decision.

(2) The precautionary principle has been followed in a number of later cases. In *Pfizer Animal Health S.A. v Council and Alpharma Inc v Council* (Cases T-13/99 and T-70/99) the CFI upheld the Council's decision to ban certain antibiotics as additives in animal feed, confirming that preventive measures may be taken before the reality and seriousness of the risk is fully apparent. There must, however, be a real

risk. The CFI acknowledged that the degree of risk cannot be set at zero. Before taking any preventive measure, public authorities must carry out a risk assessment involving both a scientific component (as thorough a scientific assessment as possible taking account of the degree of urgency) and a political component ("risk management" involving a decision by the authorities on the measures deemed appropriate according to the degree of risk). In *Artegodan GmbH v Commission* (Cases T-74/00 etc.) the CFI annulled Commission decisions ordering the withdrawal of marketing authorisation for anti-obesity drugs. After finding that the Commission was not competent to adopt the decisions as competence remained with the Member States, it went on to consider validity. The CFI held that the conditions for withdrawal of marketing authorisation must be interpreted in accordance with the general principle of protection of public health. Applying the precautionary principle where there is scientific uncertainty, the Court found that mere changes in scientific criterion for assessing the efficacy of a medical product justify withdrawal of a marketing authorisation only if those changes are supported by new data.

Key Principle: **Restrictions on imports and exports may be justified on grounds of the protection of national treasures possessing artistic, historic or archaeological value.**

Commission v Italy (Re Export Tax on Art Treasures) (Case 7/68)
The Italian Government imposed a tax on the export of art treasures from Italy, claiming that such a tax would be less restrictive than an export ban. The Commission brought an action in the ECJ under Art.226 (ex 169).

Held: (ECJ) The measure was illegal under Art.25 (ex 12) (prohibition on customs duties and measures equivalent to customs duties). It could not therefore be justified under Art.30 (ex 36). [1968] E.C.R. 423.

Commentary
In the absence of definitive case law, some guidance may be found in Regulation 3911/92 (implemented by Regulation 752/93) which

seeks to impose uniform standards at borders on the export of protected cultural goods within a licensing scheme for art treasures. Directive 93/7 gives Member States the right to define their national treasures unlawfully removed abroad.

Key Principle: **Restrictions on imports and exports may be justified on grounds of the protection of industrial and commercial property.**

EMI Electrola v Patricia (Case 341/87) 1989

Patricia and other record companies sought to take advantage of the fact that the copyright to the records of Cliff Richard had expired in Denmark but not in Germany by buying recordings in Denmark and importing them for resale in Germany.

Held: (ECJ) The recordings had not been marketed by the holder of the copyright (EMI) or with his consent, even though they had been lawfully placed on the market. EMI could rely on the copyright to keep out the recordings. [1989] E.C.R. 79.

Commentary

(1) Intellectual property rights (as industrial property rights are now usually known) take forms such as trade marks, copyright, patents and design rights. They usually operate at national level to provide protection for the holder of the right on a territorial basis. It follows that such rights may impede the free movement of goods under Arts 28 and 29 (ex 28 to 30). They may also infringe the competition rules under Arts 81 and 82 (ex 85 and 86). While Art.30 (ex 36) provides an express exception for industrial property rights, it states that such prohibitions must not constitute a means of arbitrary discrimination or disguised restriction on trade between Member States. Harmonisation of intellectual property rights is proceeding steadily.

(2) There is an extensive body of case law on intellectual property in the ECJ and CFI. Space in this text does not permit a full treatment. Many cases, particularly on trade marks, concern pharmaceutical products. One example of a particularly significant decision in which the ECJ reconsidered its earlier decisions was *Bristol-Myers Squibb v*

Paranova (Joined Cases C-427, 429 & 436/93). Paranova, a parallel importer (i.e. an importer acting without the consent of the trademark holder) bought pharmaceutical products outside Denmark, repackaged them and resold them in Denmark, undercutting the trade mark holder. The ECJ accepted that the trade mark holder may oppose marketing of the product where there is a risk of damage to the contents as a result of inappropriate repackaging, as this might damage the reputation of the trade mark holder. However, the trade mark must not artificially partition the market. The trade mark holder's rights may be limited only to the extent that the repackaging undertaken by the importer was necessary to market the product in the state of import, an objective test.

(3) A number of cases on luxury goods concern international exhaustion, the principle that once goods have been put on the market by the trade mark holder or with his consent outside the area of territorial protection for the trade mark, the trade mark holder may not rely on his rights to prevent reimportation. In *Silhouette International v Hartlauer* (Case C-355/96) S, a company registered in Austria (then a member of the EEA prior to accession) made high cost spectacles and H was a cut-price distributor not permitted to distribute S's products. S sought an injunction to prevent H who had obtained a consignment of S's spectacles in Bulgaria from re-importing them into Austria. The ECJ held under Art.234, that national rules on international exhaustion in respect of products put on the market outside the EEA under that mark by the trade mark holder, or with his consent, are contrary to Art.7(1) of the Trade Marks Directive. While the ECJ reaffirmed its stance in *Sebago and Ancienne Maison Dubois v G.B.Unie* (Case C-173/98), the *Silhouette* decision has been heavily criticised.

Key Principle: **The consent of a trade mark proprietor to marketing within the EEA goods placed on the market outside the EEA must be expressed unequivocally.**

Zino Davidoff S.A. v A&G Imports; Levi Strauss & Co, Levis Strauss UK Ltd v Tesco Stores; Tesco Plc v Costco Wholesale UK Ltd (Joined Cases C-414, 415&416/99) 2001
Zino Davidoff was the proprietor of two trade marks registered in the UK and used for toiletries and cosmetic products. The

goods were sold by Davidoff within and outside the EEA. A&G acquired stocks originally placed on the market in Singapore by Davidoff or with the company's consent and imported the goods into the UK for resale.

Levi Strauss, the proprietor of the trade marks "Levi's" and "Levi 501" registered in the UK, always refused to sell their jeans to Tesco or Costco. When Tesco and Costco sold in the UK genuine Levi products obtained outside the EEA, Levi Strauss began proceedings in the UK courts for trade mark infringement. Davidoff brought a similar claim. The High Court referred questions from the various proceedings under Art.234, to elicit clarification of the exhaustion principle in the context of the trade mark directive, where goods have been placed on the market within the EEA by the proprietor or with his consent.

Held:

(1) Consent constitutes the decisive factor in the extinction of the proprietor's exclusive right to prevent third parties from importing goods bearing his trade mark.

(2) Intention to renounce the proprietor's rights must be unequivocally demonstrated. Consent must be expressed positively.

Implied consent cannot be inferred from mere silence.

Commentary
Davidoff and *Silhouette* demonstrate the continuing power of the trade mark holder to exert rights which make it difficult for the consumer to obtain cheaply priced imports from parallel traders.

9. FREE MOVEMENT OF CAPITAL

Key Principle: **All restrictions on the free movement of capital between Member States are prohibited: Art.56(1) (ex 73b) EC.**

Ministerio Fiscal v Aldo Bordessa (Cases C-358 & 416/93) 1995 Various Spanish and Italian nationals were charged with attempting to take out of Spain more money than was permitted under exchange control laws without prior authorisation. The Spanish court made an Art.234 (ex 177) reference to the ECJ.

Held: (ECJ) Art.1 of Directive 88/361 prohibiting all restrictions on the free movement of capital is directly effective from July 1, 1990. Member States may require persons crossing borders to declare their assets but may not require a prior administrative authorisation, such a requirement being disproportionate. [1995] E.C.R. I-361.

Commentary

(1) Directive 88/361 was adopted as part of the single market programme to eliminate the remaining barriers to the free movement of capital. The original provision in the Treaty of Rome (old Art.67(1)) was not directly effective. The Maastricht Treaty incorporated the wording of Directive 88/361 into a revised Art.73b, so the revised Treaty Article is also directly effective: see Emilio (below). Arts 67–73 of the Treaty of Rome were repealed by the Maastricht Treaty and replaced by Art.73b(g), with effect from January 1, 1994. These new provisions were renumbered 56–60, except for old Arts 73a and e, which were repealed.

(2) In *Sans de Lera* (Case C-163, 165 & 250/94) the ECJ held that Art.56 (ex 73(b)), which provides for the free movement of capital between the EU and third states, is also directly effective.

Key Principle: **National laws prohibiting the export of currency without prior authorisation are illegal under the EC Treaty.**

Ministerio Fiscalo v Emilio (Cases C-163, 164 and 250/94) 1995
Various individuals took money in excess of the permitted limits out of Spain to Turkey and Switzerland. They were prosecuted under Spanish law. An Art.234 (ex 177) reference was made to clarify the legal status of Art.73b (now Art.56) EC.

Held: (ECJ) Member States may not require prior authorisation before currency is exported, but may require a declaration of assets. [1995] 1 C.M.L.R. 631.

Commentary

(1) *Emilio* was decided after the Maastricht amendments to the Treaty. It upholds the decision in *Bordessa*. Thus Art.56(1) (ex 73b) must be regarded as directly effective. Article 58 (ex 73d) allows derogations on grounds of public policy and public security, provided they do not constitute an arbitrary discrimination or a disguised restriction on the free movement of capital and payments.

(2) *Emilio* extends the principle of the free movement of capital to third countries (i.e. non-Member States). However, note that Art.60 (ex 73g) empowers the EC and Member States to take emergency measures to restrict capital movements to such countries.

Key Principle: **The free movement of capital is subject to the right of Member States to take measures in the field of taxation and in the prudent supervision of financial institutions: Art.58(1)(b) (ex 73d).**

Commission v Belgium (Case C-478/98) 2000
In 1995 the Belgian government adopted a law prohibiting Belgian residents from subscribing to securities of a loan on the eurobond market, claiming that the measure ensured effective fiscal supervision by preventing tax evasion. The Commission brought enforcement proceedings under Art.226.

Held: (1) The prohibition contravened the principle of proportionality.

(2) A general presumption of tax evasion does not justify a measure which infringes the Treaty.

Key Principle: **The free movement of capital is subject to the right of Member States to take measures which are justified on grounds of public policy or public security: Art.58(1)(b) (ex 73d).**

Association Eglise de Scientologie de Paris, Scientology International Reserves Trust v The Prime Minister (Case C-54/99) 2000
The applicants asked the Prime Minister of France on February 1, 1996 to repeal various legislative provisions laying down a system of prior authorisation for direct foreign investments. Having found that legislative amendments on February 14, 1996 amounted to a system of prior authorisation, they interpreted this as a refusal by the Prime Minister to comply with their request and mounted a challenge in the Conseil d'Etat. A reference was made to the ECJ under Art.234 to clarify the meaning of (old) Art.73d in such circumstances.

Held: Art.73d (now 58(1)(b)) precludes a system of prior authorisation for direct foreign investments which confines itself to defining in general terms the affected investments as those which represent a threat to public policy and public security, with the result that the persons concerned cannot identify the circumstances in which prior authorisation is required.

Commentary
The derogation in Art.58(1)(b) is interpreted strictly and is subject to the requirement that the measures do not amount to arbitrary discrimination or a disguised restriction on the free movement of capital between Member States: Art.58(3).

The third stage of EMU began on January 1, 1999 when the euro was introduced as the single currency under the control of the European Central Bank for the participating states. The 10 new Member States will not adopt the euro immediately, but will have to wait until they can demonstrate that their economies have converged with those of the Eurozone.

10. FREE MOVEMENT OF WORKERS

Workers

Key Principle: **Freedom of movement for workers shall be secured within the Community: Art.39 (ex 48).**

Key Principle: **A worker is someone who performs services for and under the direction of another in return for remuneration during a certain period of time.**

Lawrie-Blum v Land Baden Wurttemberg (Case 66/85) 1986
Lawrie-Blum, a United Kingdom national, passed the first examination to qualify as a teacher in Germany. However, she was refused admission to the period of probationary service which must be undertaken before the second examination because she was not a German national. While Lawrie-Blum claimed that the refusal on nationality grounds infringed Art.39(2) (ex 48(2)), the Land argued that a probationary teacher was not a "worker" under Art.39 (ex 48).

Held: (ECJ) A trainee teacher who, under the direction and supervision of the school authorities, is undergoing a period of service in preparation for the teaching profession, during which he provides services by giving lessons and receives remuneration must be regarded as a worker under Art.39(1) (ex 48(1)), irrespective of the legal nature of the employment relationship. [1986] E.C.R. 2121.

Commentary

(1) The meaning of "worker" must be defined in EC, not national terms.

(2) Art.39 does not give rights to EC nationals working in their own countries. Thus a Surinamese mother was not entitled to join her son, a Dutch national, in the Netherlands where he was working: *Morson v The Netherlands* (Cases 35 & 36/82) 1982.

Work and economic activity

Key Principle: **The rules governing the free movement of workers only apply to individuals who pursue or wish to pursue an economic activity.**

Levin v Staatssecretaris van Justitie (Case 53/81) 1982

Mrs Levin, a United Kingdom national married to a non-EC national, sought a permit to reside in the Netherlands. She was refused on the ground that, as she was not gainfully employed, she could not be considered as a "favoured EEC citizen". She appealed against the decision through the Dutch courts, meanwhile working part-time as a waitress. An Art.234 (ex 177) reference was made.

Held: (ECJ) The expression "worker" covers those who undertake part-time work, even where they are paid at a lower rate than the national guaranteed minimum, provided the work is genuine and not marginal or ancillary. [1982] E.C.R. 1035.

Commentary

Part-time employment supplemented by public assistance was considered to be "work" in *Kempf v Staatssecretaris van Justitie* (Case 139/85) 1986. In *Steymann v Staatssecretaris van Justitie* (Case 196/87) 1988, a member of a religious community who received pocket money and keep was a worker because commercial activity was a genuine and inherent part of membership. Contrast with *Bettray v Staatssecretaris van Justitie* (Case 344/87) 1989 where subsidised work carried out by a former drug addict at a rehabilitation centre was not work as it was not a genuine economic activity.

Workers Families

Key Principle: **Member States shall facilitate the admission of workers' families: Art.10(2), Regulation 1612/68, provided the worker has accommodation available at a standard considered normal for national workers in the area concerned: Art.10(3).**

Commission v Germany (Case 249/86) 1989

Germany had adopted legislation which made the renewal of residence permits for family members conditional on their living in housing considered normal, not only at the time of arrival but throughout the duration of their stay. The Commission brought an action against Germany under Art.226 (ex 169).

Held: (ECJ) Germany was in breach of Art.10(3) of Regulation 1612/68. The obligation applies to the time of arrival of each family member, after which the migrant worker must be treated on the same basis as a worker of the state concerned. [1989] E.C.R. 1263.

Commentary

(1) Free movement of workers would be meaningless if workerscould not install their families with them. Regulation 1612/68 recognised the right of installation for workers' families (defined as the worker's spouse, descendants under 21 and dependent relatives in the ascendant line of the worker or his spouse): Art.10(1) repealed by Directive 2004/38. See *R. v Immigration Appeal Tribunal, Ex p. Surinder Singh* (Case C-370/90) (Art.10(1) applies to family members of a worker returning to his home state).

(2) Directive 2004/38 is due for implementation by April 30, 2006. It gives Union citizens and their family members the right to move freely and to reside throughout the territories of the Member States. It amends Regulation 1612/68, repeals most previous relevant secondary legislation (Directives 68/360, 90/364 and 365, 93/96) and replaces Directive 64/221.

(3) Workers and their families may remain permanently in thestate of residence, even after the death of the worker, under Regulation 1251/70. See new Art.12 of Regulation 2004/38.

Spouses

Key Principle: **The spouse of the worker is entitled to install himself or herself with the worker in the territory of the state where the EC national is working.**

Netherlands v Reed (Case 59/85) 1986
Ms Reed lived with her partner in the Netherlands. Both were United Kingdom nationals but only Ms Reed's partner was

employed. After living in the Netherlands for a year, Ms Reed sought a residence permit. She claimed that social developments in the Netherlands had reached the stage where an unmarried couple living together in a stable relationship should be treated as husband and wife for EC immigration purposes. The Dutch court made an Art.234 (ex 177) reference to the ECJ.

Held: (ECJ) Social developments in a single Member State cannot affect the development of EC law; thus relationships outside marriage cannot entitle the individual concerned to be treated as a spouse. However, under Dutch law an alien who had a stable relationship with a Dutch national was permitted to reside in the country under certain conditions. Applying the principle of non-discrimination, an alien should be granted the same rights of residence whether cohabiting with a Dutch national or an EC national. [1986] E.C.R. 1283.

Commentary

(1) Ms Reed gained the right to reside in the Netherlands because there was a Dutch law giving residence rights to aliens in specific circumstances which, under Art.7 EEC (now Art.12 EC) was extended to her.

(2) The position of cohabitees will change in some Member States when Directive 2004/38 comes into effect in May 2006. The Directive redefines 'spouse' to include the partner with whom the Union citizen has a registered partnership where the legislation of the Member States treats registered partnerships as equivalent to marriage. Under Art.3(2), Member States are required to facilitate entry and residence of family members where serious health grounds strictly require the personal care of the family member by the Union citizen and of partners with whom the Union citizen has a duly attested durable relationship.

Key Principle: **Separation does not dissolve the marital relationship for the purpose of EC residence rights.**

Diatta v Land Berlin (Case 267/83) 1985
A woman of Senegalese nationality married a French national. The couple lived in Germany where the husband was

employed. After a year they separated with the intention of becoming divorced. After Mrs Diatta's temporary residence permit expired she applied for an extension. The application was refused on the ground that, as she no longer lived with her husband, she was not a family member of an EC national.

Held: (ECJ) Art.10(3) of Regulation 1612/68 does not imply that the family must live under the same roof permanently. The marital relationship cannot be regarded as dissolved so long as it has not been terminated by the competent authority. [1985] E.C.R. 567.

Commentary
In a decision which has been much criticised, the House of Lords attempted to apply Diatta in *R. v Secretary of State for the Home Department, Ex p. Sandhu* (1985) (HL). Sandhu, an Indian national, married a German woman. The couple moved to the United Kingdom where a son was born. The marriage broke down, after which Mrs Sandhu and the child moved to Germany. Sandhu visited his family in Germany, but was denied re-entry to the United Kingdom on the ground that his residence rights had ended when his wife left the United Kingdom. The House of Lords considered that the position was covered by Diatta, refused to make an Art.234 (ex 177) reference and upheld the decision of the immigration authorities to deny entry. Article 13(2) of the Directive provides that divorce, annulment or termination of the registered partnership does not necessarily lead to loss of residence rights for family members, etc.

Rights of entry

Key Principle: **Workers who are EC nationals and their families are entitled, on production of a passport or valid identity card, to enter the territory of other Member States in order to work.**

Procureur du Roi v Royer (Case 48/75)
R, a French national with a conviction for procuring, was prosecuted with (and later convicted of) illegal entry into Belgium. R had not complied with administrative formalities on entry into Belgium where his wife ran a dance hall. He was expelled on the grounds that his personal conduct showed that

he was a danger to public policy and that he had not observed the conditions for aliens. An Art.234 (ex 177) reference was made.

Held: (ECJ) The right for EC nationals to enter the territory of another Member State covers the right to enter in search of work or to rejoin a spouse or family. Failure by a national of a Member State to complete the legal formalities on access, movement and residence, does not justify expulsion. [1976] E.C.R. 497.

Commentary

(1) In *R. v Immigration Appeal Tribunal, Ex p. Antonissen* (Case C-292/89) 1991 the ECJ found that deportation of a convicted drug dealer after six months' residence in the United Kingdom without finding work did not contravene EC law, unless the individual concerned could provide evidence that he was continuing to seek employment and had a genuine chance of finding work.

(2) Involuntary unemployment is not a ground for deportation.

(3) In *MRAX v Belgium* (Case C-459/99) the ECJ held that third country nationals who are married to EC nationals should possess a visa when crossing the border into other Member States. However, in view of the principle of proportionality, a Member State may not send back such an individual who has not got a passport, visa or identity card, provided he can prove his identity and married status, and that he does not represent a threat to public policy, public security or public health under Directive 64/221.

(4) See now Art.5 of Directive 2004/38.

Equality of treatment

Key Principle: **Freedom of movement entails the abolition of discrimination based on nationality between workers of Member States as regards employment, remuneration and other conditions of work and employment: Art.39(2) (ex 48(2)).**

Eligibility for employment

Key Principle: **EC nationals are entitled to take up and pursue employment in the territory of another Member State under the same conditions as the nationals of the host state: Art.1, Regulation 1612/68.**

Commission v France (Case 167/73) 1974

The French Code du Travail Maritime specified that a proportion of the crew of merchant ships must be French nationals. While this proportion had been set at three French crew members to one non-French crew member, the French Government claimed that it had not in practice been applied against EC nationals. The Commission brought enforcement proceedings against France under Art.169 for breach of Art.48 of the Treaty and Art.4 of Regulation 1612/68 (prohibition on restriction by number of percentage of EC nationals in a particular activity or area).

Held: (ECJ) In failing to amend the Code in relation to EC nationals from other Member States, France was in breach of Art.39 (ex 48) of the Treaty and Art.4 of the Regulation. [1974] E.C.R. 359.

Commentary

While a state may not prescribe special recruitment procedures, limit advertising or otherwise hinder the recruitment of non-nationals, it may impose conditions relating to linguistic competence: *Groener v Minister for Education* (Case 397/87) (requirement for teachers in vocational schools in Ireland to be proficient in the Irish language permissible in the light of national policy on promotion of the Irish language).

Key Principle: **The regulation of professional sporting activities is subject to the principle of equality.**

Union des Associations Europeenes de Football v Jean-Marc Bosman (Case C-415/93) 1995

UEFA, which regulates national football associations, had adopted two rules for implementation nationally. The first rule, incorporated into players' contracts, allowed national football clubs to impose a transfer fee when a player moved to a new club. Without a fee players could not change clubs. The second rule restricted the number of non-national players in a national club to three. Bosman, a Belgian footballer, was unable to move from a Belgian to a French club because the transfer fee was rejected. He sued the Belgian club, the Belgian national football association and UEFA, claiming that the rules infringed Art.39(2) (ex 48(2)).

Held: (ECJ) Transfer rules such as those adopted by UEFA directly affect players' access to the employment markets in other Member States and constitute an obstacle to the free movement of workers under Art.39 (ex 48). Rules restricting the rights of EC nationals to take part in professional football matches also amount to an obstacle to free movement. Such rules are covered by Art.48(2) and by Art.4 of Regulation 1612/68 (prohibition of quotas based on nationality: see pp.100–101 above) implementing Art.39(2) (ex 48(2)). [1996] All E.R. (EC) 97.

Commentary

(1) Discrimination on grounds of nationality in professional and semi-professional sport contravenes both Art.39 and Art.6 of the EC Treaty (now Art.12 EC), the principle of non-discrimination: *Dona v Mantero* (Case 13/76) 1976. See also *UNECTEF v Heylens* (Case 222/86) 1987.

(2) It is, however, legitimate to restrict membership of a team on grounds of nationality for non-economic reasons (e.g. to represent a particular country in an international match). See also *Deliège* (Cases C-51/96 & C-191/97).

Equality in employment

Key Principle: **Non-national EC workers may not be treated differently from national workers on account of nationality in relation to conditions of employment, dismissal, reinstatement or re-employment.**

Sotgiu v Deutsche Bundespost (Case 152/73) 1974
Sotgiu was an Italian national living in Germany where he was employed by the Federal Post Office. His family remained in

Italy. Under a collective wages agreement he was entitled to a separation allowance. However, the allowance was payable at a lower rate for workers whose normal residence was abroad than for those whose home was in Germany. He challenged the rate in the German courts, which made an Art.177 reference.

Held: (ECJ) A separation allowance falls within the concept of "conditions of employment and work" under Art.7(1) of Regulation 1612/68. [1974] E.C.R. 153.

Commentary
  (1) Equal treatment is now governed by Art.24 of Regulation 2004/38.
  (2) The ECJ considered in Sotgiu that it made no difference whether the payment was voluntary or compulsory. Once the state had decided to pay the allowance to its own nationals, it must extend the same benefit to EC nationals from other Member States.

Social and tax advantages

Key Principle: **Non-national EC workers are entitled to the same social and tax advantages as national workers.**

Fiorini (Cristini) v SNCF (Case 32/75) 1976
An Italian widow living in France claimed for a special fare reduction card which the French railways (SNCF) provided to the parents of large families, this concession having previously been claimed by her husband. The claim was refused because Mrs Fiorini was not a French national. She challenged the refusal in the French courts, which made an Art.234 (ex 177) reference.

Held: **(ECJ) Art.7(2) of Regulation 1612/68 applied to all social or tax advantages, irrespective of whether they derive from the contract of employment. As the family were entitled to remain in France (under Regulation 1251/70) they were also entitled under Art.7(2) to equal "social advantage". [1975] E.C.R. 1085.**

Commentary

  (1) See now Art.24 of Directive 2004/38.

(2) In *Castelli v ONPTS* (Case 261/83) (1984) a guaranteed minimum income for old people, paid to an Italian widow living with her retired son in Belgium, was held to be a "social advantage". See also *Reina v Landeskreditbank Baden-Wurttenberg* (Case 65/81) (interest-free loan granted on childbirth by a credit institution incorporated under public law to low income families in order to stimulate the birth rate is a social advantage).

(3) EC nationals employed or self-employed in another Member State are entitled to aggregate their periods of social security contributions in different Member States and receive benefits in whichever state they are resident: Regulation 1408/71.

Maintenance grants and education

Key Principle: **A maintenance grant to cover education is a social advantage.**

Lair v University of Hanover (Case 39/86) 1988
Mrs Lair was a French national living in Germany for five years, during which time she had worked but had also been involuntarily unemployed from time to time. Having enrolled on a language course at the University of Hanover, she applied for a maintenance grant (an interest-free loan) from the German authorities. Her application was refused on the ground that she had not been employed in Germany for five years, a requirement only applied to foreign applicants. She challenged the refusal in the German courts, which made an Art.234 (ex 177) reference.

Held: (ECJ) (1) While Art.7 of the EEC Treaty (now Art.12 EC) applies to grants for access to education (e.g. tuition fees), it does not apply to maintenance grants. A maintenance grant is a "social advantage" under Art.7(2) of Regulation 1612/68, provided the course in question is vocational.

(2) For an immigrant to retain the status of "worker" there must be a connection between his previous career and choice of study. Member States may not lay down minimum periods of residence or employment, as the concept of "EC worker" is a Community one, which cannot be limited by national law. [1988] E.C.R. 3161.

Commentary

(1) Similar issues were raised in *Brown* (Case 197/86), decided by the ECJ on the same day as *Lair*. In *Brown* the applicant was a student with dual British-French nationality. Having been brought up in France he had been offered a place to study electrical engineering at Cambridge. To gain practical experience, Brown undertook pre-university industrial training with a firm in Scotland, such training being open only to students holding the offer of a degree place. Brown's application to the United Kingdom Government for a grant for fees and maintenance was refused, as he had not lived in the United Kingdom for the required three years. The ECJ held under Art.234 (ex 177) that while the applicant's pre-university industrial experience gave him the status of worker, he had obtained the work only because of his university place. He was not, therefore, entitled to a grant under Regulation 1612/68.

(2) The rulings in *Brown* and *Lair* should be read subject to the recent decision of the ECJ in *Bidar* (Case C-209/93) (below).

Key Principle: **The entitlement of students who are studying in another Member State to access to non-contributory benefits should not be made subject to a condition which is not applied to the nationals of the host state.**

Grzelczyk v Centre Public d'Aide Sociale d'Ottignies-Louvain-la-Neuve (CPAS) (Case C-184/99) 2001
G, a French national, was a student of physical education at a university in Belgium where he was resident. For the first three years of his course he supplemented his income through part-time work and credit. In his fourth and final year he applied to the CPAS for payment of the 'minimex', the minimum subsistence allowance. The CPAS was denied reimbursement of the allowance by the Belgian state authorities on the ground that G did not satisfy the nationality requirement. G challenged the decision before the Labour Tribunal which made a reference to the ECJ under Art.234 to clarify the meaning of Regulation 1612/68 and the relevance of the concepts of European citizenship and non-discrimination.

Held: (1) The case is concerned solely with discrimination on grounds of nationality.

(2) A Union citizen lawfully resident in another Member Statemay rely on Art.12 (ex 6) in all areas covered by EC law (*Martínez Sala*).

(3) Arts 12 (ex 6) and 17 (ex 8) of the Treaty preclude entitlement to a non-contributory benefit such as the minimex from being made conditional, in relation to nationals from Member States other than the host state where they are legally resident, on falling within Regulation 1612/68 where no such condition applies to nationals of the host state.

Commentary

The ECJ stated in *Grzelczyk* that "Union citizenship is destined to be the fundamental status of nationals of Member States, enabling those who find themselves in the same situation to enjoy the same treatment in law irrespective of their nationality, subject to such exceptions as are expressly provided for." It commented that pursuit by a Union citizen of university studies in a Member State other than the state of which he is a national cannot, of itself, deprive him of the possibility of relying on the prohibition of all discrimination on grounds of nationality laid down in Art.12 (ex 6) of the Treaty.

Key principle: **Students may be required to demonstrate a degree of integration into the society of the Member State before being granted a subsidized loan or grant.**

Dany Bidar (Case C-209/03) 2005

The applicant was a French national, resident in the UK since he arrived in 1998 with his mother, who required medical treatment. He attended school in London and then began a degree in Economics at University College London. Although he received a maintenance grant, he was refused a student loan on the grounds that he was not settled in the UK. The UK court referred questions to the ECJ for interpretation.

Held: (ECJ) EU citizens lawfully resident in another Member State were covered by the principle of non-discrimination in

Art.12 of the Treaty for the purpose of assistance for students, whether as a subsidized loan or as a grant to cover maintenance costs, provided the students have demonstrated "a certain degree of integration into the society of that State". This may be satisfied by showing that the student in question had lived in the Member State for "a certain length of time".

Commentary

(1) Although the ECJ referred to *Brown* and *Lair* in its ruling, it found that the position had changed with the introduction of Union citizenship, enabling the application of the principle of non-discrimination to apply.
(2) For further caselaw on Union citizenship, see pp.137–139.

Key Principle: **Children of migrant workers must be admitted to the host state's educational, apprenticeship and vocational training under the same conditions as the nationals of the host state.**

Casagrande v Landeshauptstadt Munchen (Case 9/74) 1974

C was the child of a deceased Italian national who had been working in Germany. His application for a monthly educational grant was rejected by the Munich authorities because the grant was payable only to German nationals, stateless persons and aliens with asylum. The Bavarian Administrative Court made an Art.234 (ex 177) reference to the ECJ.

Held: (ECJ) In providing that the children of migrant workers must be admitted to educational courses under the same conditions as the nationals of the host state, Art.12 of Regulation 1612/68 covers not only admission but also general measures to facilitate admission (i.e. grants and loans). [1974] E.C.R. 773.

Commentary

Where a national of a Member State is employed or self-employed in another Member State, his spouse and children under 21 (or dependent) were entitled to take up any activity as an employed person in that state even if they are not EC nationals: Art.11, Regulation 1612/68. Regulation 1612/68 was amended by Directive 2004/38. See Art.24 on equal treatment.

Employment in the public service

Key Principle: **The principle of free movement in Art.39 does
not apply to employment in the public service: Art.39(4).**

Commission v Belgium (Re Public Employees) (Case 149/79) 1980

A wide range of posts in the public service in Belgium were
advertised as reserved for Belgian nationals: posts in the
National Railway Company, the National Local Railway Company, the City of Brussels and the Commune of Auderghem.
The Commission brought Art.226 (ex 169) proceedings against
Belgium which sought to invoke Art.39(4) (ex 48(4)) as a
defence.

Held: (ECJ) To be covered by Art.39(4) (ex 48(4)) employment
must involve direct or indirect participation in the exercise of
powers conferred by public law and duties designed to safeguard the general interests of the state or other public authorities. [1982] E.C.R. 1845.

Commentary

(1) The distinction between posts outside and posts within the
exception does not seem entirely logical. Posts outside
Art.39(4) have been held by the ECJ to include nurses in
public hospitals, local authority gardeners and teachers in
public educational institutions, in contrast with local authority night-watchmen and architects who are within the
exception.

(2) In 1988 the Commission issued a notice listing occupations
which should not normally be covered by the exception:
public health services, teaching in state educational establishments, nonmilitary research in public establishments and
public bodies responsible for administering commercial services. Arguably, only high level posts with a particular
allegiance to the state should be covered (e.g. the police and
the judiciary).

(3) In *Commission v Luxembourg* (Case C-473/93) 1996 the
ECJ found that Luxembourg was in breach of Art.39 (ex 48)
by restricting civil service and public sector employment in
relation to teaching, health, inland transport, telecommunications, water, gas and electricity, regardless of the
level of responsibility.

Derogation from the Principle of Free Movement

Key Principle: **Freedom of movement of workers may be restricted on grounds of public policy, public health and public security: Art.39(3) (ex 48(3)).**

Key Principle: **Measures taken on grounds of public policy of public security shall be based exclusively on the personal conduct of the individual concerned: Art.27(2) of Directive 2004/38.**

Van Duyn v Home Office (No.2) (Case 41/74) 1974

Ms Van Duyn, a Dutch national, sought to take up employment for the Church of Scientology in the United Kingdom. At the time the Church of Scientology was not illegal in the United Kingdom but was considered by the Government to be socially harmful. She was refused entry to take up the post on grounds that it was undesirable for anyone to enter the country to work for the Church of Scientology. Ms Van Duyn sought judicial review in the High Court, which made an Art.177 reference.

Held: (ECJ) (1) Art.39(1) and (2) (ex 48(1) and (2)) are directly effective in the national courts from the end of the transitional period (1961).

(2) Directive 64/221 (see now Directive 2004/38) is also directly effective.

(3) A Member State, in imposing restrictions on grounds of public policy, is entitled to take account, as personal conduct, of an individual's association with an organisation which the Member State considers socially harmful, even where no equivalent restriction is placed on the nationals of the host state. [1974] E.C.R. 1337.

Commentary

(1) Directive 64/221 is repealed by Directive 2004/38.

(2) The derogations in Directive 64/221 applied not only to workers but also to all categories of EC nationals including those exercising the right of establishment or provision of services in another Member State. "Public policy" is a

translation of the French expression "ordre public" and is closer to the United Kingdom legal concept of "public order". The derogation must be strictly interpreted, although national authorities have discretion within the limits of the Treaty and secondary legislation. "Public security" is rarely invoked, but overlaps with the concept of public policy. Diseases that might endanger public health, public policy or public security were listed in an Annex to the Directive.

(2) *Van Duyn* appears to allow a dual standard whereby Member States may impose stricter requirements on EC nationals entering the country than on its own nationals. In Adoui and *Cornuaille v Belgian State* (Joined Cases 115 & 116/81) the ECJ upheld the ruling in *Van Duyn* in the context of a refusal to grant two French prostitutes residence permits in Belgium where prostitution is not illegal. However, the Court added that in such circumstances a state must not base the exercise of its powers on assessments of conduct that would have the effect of applying an arbitrary distinction to the nationals of other Member States.

Key Principle: **The public policy proviso may only be invoked where there is a genuine and sufficiently serious threat to one of the fundamental interests of society.**

R. v Bouchereau (Case 30/77) 1977

B, a French national working in the United Kingdom, was convicted of the unlawful possession of drugs in 1976. Six months earlier he had been convicted of another offence of possession and had been conditionally discharged for 12 months. The magistrates court, before recommending deportation, made an Art.177 reference to clarify the meaning of "public policy".

Held: (ECJ) (1) A recommendation to deport is a measure under Art.3 of Directive 64/221.

(2) Previous criminal convictions may only be taken into account where they provide evidence of personal conduct amounting to a present threat.

(3) Recourse to the concept of public policy presupposes the existence of a genuine and sufficiently serious threat to the requirements of public policy affecting one of the fundamental interests of society. [1977] E.C.R. 1999.

Commentary

(1) The threat must derive from the conduct of the individual in question and is not to discourage others. In *Bonsignore v Oberstadtdirektor der Stadt Koln* (Case 67/74) 1975, an Italian national living in Germany accidentally shot dead his brother. He was convicted but no sentence was imposed. B appealed against his deportation order to the local administrative court which made an Art.234 (ex 177) reference. *Held*: (ECJ) deportation may not be ordered for reasons of a general preventive nature. Failure to observe administrative formalities does not provide grounds for deportation: *Royer* (Case 48/75) (see p.111).

(2) Procedural rights covering the right of re-entry, therequirement to specify the grounds for decision and entitlement to remedies are also provided by Directive 64/221.

(3) It should be noted that Directive 64/221 will be repealed and replaced by Directive 2004/38 in April 2006. The new provisions are similar but specify (in Art.27(2)) that measures taken on grounds of public policy or public security shall comply with the principle of proportionality and shall be based exclusively on the personal conduct of the individual concerned. Criminal convictions are not automatically grounds for taking such measures.

Key Principle: **Automatic expulsion from the territory of a Member State for possession of illegal drugs for personal use is not justified under Directive 64/221.**

Donatella Calfa (Case C-348/96) [1999]
Mrs Calfa, an Italian national on holiday in Crete, had been charged by the Greek authorities with possession of prohibited drugs for her personal use. As the recipient of services under Art.49 (ex 59) (see Ch.11) she would have been entitled to move around the EC on holiday, subject to the derogations in Directive 64/221. If convicted, she faced an automatic life ban from reentering Greece under Greek law. The Greek court referred questions to the ECJ under Art.234 (ex 177) to clarify the meaning of the Directive in such circumstances.

Held: (ECJ) The ECJ ruled that automatic expulsion following a criminal conviction infringed Directive 64/221 because it took no account of the personal conduct of the offender or the extent to which he or she posed a threat to public policy. [1999] E.C.R. I-1919.

Commentary

(1) *Calfa* reaffirms the principle in earlier decisions such as *Bouchereau* and *Bonsignore* that the personal conduct of the individual and the nature of the threat must be considered before any expulsion may be justified under Directive 64/221.

(2) An expulsion decision may not be taken against Union citizens, unless the decision is based on imperative grounds of public security, as defined by Member States, if they have resided in the host Member State for the previous 10 years (Art.28(3) of Directive 2004/38).

Key Principle: **A Member State may not impose territorial restrictions on residence on a national from another Member State except in circumstances where such prohibitions may be imposed on its own nationals.**

Rutili v Minister of the Interior (Case 36/75) 1975

R, an Italian national and trade union activist, was required by the French authorities to reside in specified regions in France. He sought annulment of the decision on residence before the French courts which made an Art.234 (ex 177) reference to the ECJ.

Held: (ECJ) Measures restricting the right of residence which are limited to part of the national territory may not be imposed on EC nationals from other Member States except where they could also be applied to nationals of the state concerned. [1975] E.C.R. 1219.

Commentary

The ECJ in *Rutili* describes Directive 64/221 (Arts 2 and 3) as a manifestation of the principle in the European Convention of Human Rights that no restrictions in the interest of national security or public safety shall be placed on rights secured by the

Convention other than those which are necessary to protect those interests in a democratic society.

Key Principle: **Where there is no right of appeal to a court of law, a decision refusing renewal of a residence permit order- ing expulsion of an EC national from another Member State shall not normally be taken without an opinion from a competent authority of the host country: Art.9, Directive 64/221.**

R. v Secretary of State for the Home Department, Ex p.Gal- lagher (Case C-175/94) 1996.
G, an Irish national, had a previous conviction for a firearm offence. He was deported from the UK on grounds of suspicion of involvement with terrorist activities.

Held: Art.9 requires an opinion to be obtained from a compe- tent, independent body before deportation. [1993] E.C.R. I-3545.

Commentary
(1) Gallagher later brought a claim for state liability against the UK Government arising from his deportation. The Court of Appeal considered that waiting for G to make his repres- entations and for the independent monitor to report before deportation would not have been in been in G's interests as he would have been detained in custody. G was able to make representations to the UK Government after deporta- tion. A report was obtained retrospectively from the inde- pendent monitor, supporting the decision to deport. The CA held that the breach was not sufficiently serious for G to succeed; while the breach was "manifest" it was not "grave" (See Ch.1).

(2) Directive 64/221 is repeated by Directive 2004/38. See now Article 31 for procedural safeguards on expulsion decisions.

11. RIGHT OF ESTABLISHMENT AND FREEDOM TO PROVIDE SERVICES

The right of establishment

Key Principle: **Restrictions on the freedom of establishment of nationals of a Member State in the territory of another Member State shall be prohibited: Art.43(1) (ex 52(1)).**

Reyners v Belgian State (Case 2/74) 1974

Reyners was a Dutch national living in Belgium where he wished to be admitted to practise the profession of "avocat", having gained the appropriate academic qualification. He was prevented by a requirement that only Belgian nationals could be admitted. He challenged the Belgian law in the Conseil d'Etat which made an Art.234 (ex 177) reference to the ECJ.

Held: (ECJ) Art.43 (ex 52) became directly effective by the end of the transitional period and was not dependent on the adoption of further directives under the General Programme. [1974] E.C.R. 631.

Commentary

(1) The right of establishment under Art.43 entitles an EC national who is established in one Member State to set up a business in another state on the same conditions as a national of the state concerned. EC nationals may take up and pursue activities as self-employed persons and set up and manage undertakings. They may also establish an agency, branch or subsidiary in another state. The right applies both to natural and legal persons (companies incorporated in a Member State). There is considerable overlap between the right of establishment and the provision of services: see below.

(2) The transitional period ended in December 1961. The General Programme for the abolition of restrictions on the freedom of establishment was adopted in 1961 under Art.47 (ex 57) EC. In 1974 the Commission decided that further

directives on the right of establishment were unnecessary. Note that it was also held in Reyners that the profession of advocate is not an activity connected with state authority under Art.45 (ex 55) and is thus not excluded from Art.43 (ex 52).

(3) In *Commission v UK* (Case C-246/89) (see Ch.1, p.7) United Kingdom requirements based on nationality and domicile for registration of fishing vessels were discriminatory. They infringed Arts 43 (ex 52) and 49 (ex 59) (freedom to provide services) and resulted in an order against the United Kingdom Government in *Factortame III* (Case C-48/93) to compensate the Spanish fishermen who suffered financial loss.

(4) Note the decision of the ECJ in *Metalallgesellschaft v Inland Revenue Commissioners* (Cases C-379/98 & C-410/98) in relation to Art.43 (ex 52) (see Ch.1, p.14).

Key Principle: **Even where there is no discrimination on grounds of nationality, national requirements on qualifications may hinder the right of establishment under Art.43 (ex 52).**

Vlassopoulou v Ministerium for Justiz, Bundes-und Europaangelegenheiten Baden-Wurttemberg (Case C-340/89)
V, a Greek lawyer and member of the Athens Bar, sought admission as a lawyer in Germany. She challenged the German demand to examine her qualifications for comparison with national requirements.

Held: (ECJ) A Member State may require the examination of an individual's qualifications from another Member State before admission to the legal profession to determine the extent to which the knowledge and qualification attested by the diploma correspond to those of the host state. [1993] 2 C.M.L.R. 221.

Commentary
Where a diploma corresponds only partially, the individual may be required to prove that he or she has acquired the necessary knowledge and qualifications. Contrast *Vlassopoulou* with *Thieffry v Conseil de L'Ordre des Avocats a la Cour de Paris* (Case 71/76) in

which a Belgian lawyer with academic qualifications recognised as equivalent, was refused admission to the Paris Bar because he lacked a French diploma. *Held*: (ECJ) such a requirement breached Art.43 (ex 52). See also *Patrick v Ministre des Affaires Culturelles* (Case 11/77) where a United Kingdom trained architect could not be prevented from practising in France where his qualifications were recognised as equivalent.

Key Principle: **Rights of establishment and the provision of services may be restricted where the limitation is objectively justified in the general interest.**

Commission v Germany (Case 205/84) 1986

German law required the providers of insurance services in the territory to be established in Germany. Prior authorisation was also required from the German authorities. The Commission brought an action against Germany in the ECJ under Art.226 (ex 169).

Held: (ECJ) The requirement for the providers of insurance services to be established in Germany infringed Art.43 (ex 52). However, the requirement for prior authorisation was justified in so far as it protected policy holders and insured persons. [1986] E.C.R. 3755.

Commentary

(1) The single market in financial services has since *Commission v Germany* and other cases been completed with the adoption of a number of directives including measures to harmonise safeguards and standards in insurance.

(2) In *Gebhard v Consiglio Dell' Ordine Degli Avvocati Procurator di Milano* (Case C-55/94) a German member of the Stuttgart Bar was subjected to disciplinary proceedings by the Milan Bar for practising in Italy using the title "avvocato". The ECJ in an Art.234 (ex 177) reference held that where national measures restrict one of the fundamental freedoms, they must be:

(a) non-discriminatory;

(b) justified by imperative requirements in the general interest;

    (c) suitable for attaining the objective;
    (d) not disproportionate.

(3) In *MacQuen v Grandvision Belgium SA* (Case C-108/96) the ECJ held that Art.43 (ex 52) does not in principle preclude a prohibition under national law which prohibits opticians from carrying out certain optical examinations where it is justified by the protection of public health.

(4) In *Wouters v Algemeine Raad van der Nederlandse Ordre van Avocaten* (Case C-309/99) the ECJ held that a national regulation prohibiting multi-disciplinary partnerships between members of the Bar and accountants was not contrary to Arts 43 and 49, since such regulations could reasonably be considered necessary for the proper practice of the legal profession as it was organised in the country concerned.

The provision of services

Qualifications and residential requirements

Key Principle: **Restrictions on the freedom to provide services shall be progressively abolished during the transitional period for EC nationals established in one Member State and providing services in another Member State: Art.49 (ex 59).**

Commission v Greece (Case C-198/89) 1991
Greek law required tourist guides accompanying tour groups from other Member States to hold a licence granted only to diploma holders who had undertaken specific training. (A separate requirement for specialised professional guides covered visits to museums and other monuments.) The Commission brought an action in the ECJ under Art.226 (ex 169) against Greece on the basis that the requirement for a licence infringed Art.49 (ex 59).

Held: (ECJ) While the general interest in the proper appreciation of the artistic and archaeological heritage of a country may justify a restriction on the provision of services, the requirement for a licence had a disproportionate effect. (It reduced the number of available tour guides, particularly those speaking the language of the tour group.) The measure infringed Art.49 (ex 59). [1991] E.C.R. I-727.

Commentary

(1) A similar requirement in relation to tourist guides in France was also found to be disproportionate in *Commission v France* (Case C-154/89).

(2) Many cases on Art.49 (ex 59) concern national requirements for professional qualifications which, without harmonisation or recognition, may severely limit both establishment and the provision of services. Directive 89/48 provides for the recognition of qualifications requiring higher education diplomas of three years or more duration where education or training is substantially the same. Where there is a substantial difference, an aptitude test or period of adaptation may be required by the host state. The principle is extended to qualifications of less than three years by Directive 92/51.

Key Principle: **Restrictions such as a residential requirement may infringe Arts 43 (ex 52) and 49 (ex 59) unless they are necessary to observe professional rules of conduct.**

Van Binsbergen v Bestuur van de Bedrifsveerniging voor de Metaalnijverheied (Case 33/74) 1974

Kortman, the legal adviser of Van B, was told that he could no longer represent his client before the Dutch courts when he moved from the Netherlands to Belgium. An Art.234 (ex 177) reference was made.

Held: (ECJ) Art.49 (ex 59) is directly effective from the end of the transitional period. A residence requirement contravenes Art.49 (ex 59) unless it is objectively justified by the need to observe professional rules of conduct. [1974] E.C.R. 1299.

Commentary

(1) The line of case law dealing with the possible objective justification of residential and other nationally based requirements, as in *Commission v Germany* (see above), is analogous to the "rule of reason" in *Cassis de Dijon*. (See p.88).

(2) Lawyers seeking to provide services in other Member States are covered by Directive 77/249 and Directive 98/5 (which seeks to make it easier for lawyers to practise on a self-

employed or salaried basis in a state other than the one in which they qualified; Directive 98/5 is subject to a challenge in the ECJ).

(3) Article 49 is subject to Directive 64/221, and in due course Directive 2004/38. In *Omega Air* (Case C-36/02) the ECJ had to consider a referral from a German court arising from an appeal against a ban on human targets imposed by Germany on a German company operating a laser targeting installation. The ECJ found that the services were covered by Art.49 (the equipment and technology were supplied by a British company). However, the ban had been imposed by the German authorities on grounds that the game posed a threat to public order as it infringed human dignity through the use of simulated killings. The derogation was therefore necessary to protect fundamental rights, even though the equipment was not illegal in the UK.

Key Principle: **Where qualifications are not covered by a specific directive and are outside Directives 89/48 and 92/51, the basic rules on recognition and equivalence continue to apply.**

Colegio Oficial de Agentes de la Propriedad Immobiliara v Aguirre, Newman and others (Case C-104/91) 1992
Newman, a United Kingdom national and member of the Royal Institute of Chartered Surveyors, applied for membership of the Colegio, the body that regulated estate agency in Spain. Having received no response, he began practising as an estate agent in Spain. He was prosecuted by the Spanish authorities in 1991 before the implementation date of Directive 89/48 on the mutual recognition of qualifications. An Art.234 (ex 177) reference was made.

Held: (ECJ) In the absence of harmonisation measures, Member States may specify the knowledge and qualifications needed to pursue a profession and to require the production of a diploma certifying the status of the holder's qualifications. [1992] E.C.R. I-3003.

Commentary
In the circumstances, Spain would have been in a position to carry out a comparative examination of knowledge and qualifica-

tions. Full reasons for a refusal to recognise qualifications must be given.

Key Principle: **Where measures have been adopted to harmonise professional qualifications, national authorities must examine the experience of an applicant to a regulated profession to evaluate post qualification experience.**

Haim v Kassenzahnarttliche Vereinigun Nordhein (Case C-319/92) 1994

H was an Italian national who had qualified as a dentist in Turkey. He had practised in both Turkey and Belgium before seeking to practise in Germany. Professional qualifications for dentistry had been harmonised in an EC directive. The German authorities refused his application on the basis that he lacked the necessary qualifications. H challenged the refusal in the German courts, claiming that it infringed Art.43 (ex 52). A reference to the ECJ was made under Art.234 (ex 177).

Held: (ECJ) Failure to examine post-qualification experience may infringe Art.43 (ex 52) where the effect is to hinder EC nationals from exercising the right of establishment. [1994] E.C.R. I-425.

Commentary

(1) After harmonisation, Member States should consider relevant post-qualification experience as well as formal qualifications.

(2) The ECJ ruled on establishment in the absence of a directive in relation to the medical profession in *Hocsman v Ministre de l'Emploi et de la Solidarité* (Case C-238/98). It held that where an EC national applies to practise in another Member State, the host state must take into account all diplomas, other evidence of formal qualifications and relevant experience, by comparing the specialised knowledge and abilities certified by those qualifications and experience with the knowledge and experience required by national rules.

(3) In *Luxembourg v EP and Council* (Case C-168/98) the ECJ dismissed the action by Luxembourg to annul Directive 98/5 on the facilitation of practice of profession of lawyer in a

state other than the state of qualification. The Court found that the Directive did not infringe old Art.52(2) (now 43), since the principle of a migrant lawyer practising in his home country title and that of a lawyer practising under professional title of the host state are not comparable.

Provision of non-professional services

Key Principle: **Art.49 (ex 59) applies to services offered for remuneration across national borders. The right to provide services may only be restricted where there are overriding reasons and the restriction is not disproportionate.**

H.M. Customs and Excise v Schindler (Case C-275/92) 1992
S, acting on behalf of four local state lotteries in Germany, sent letters from the Netherlands to the United Kingdom inviting the recipients to take part in the lotteries. They enabled purchasers to participate in the lottery on payment of the price of the ticket and were offered outside the state in which the operators were established. The Customs and Excise authorities seized the letters on the grounds that they infringed United Kingdom legislation on lotteries and gambling. Schindler challenged the seizure in the United Kingdom courts. An Art.234 (ex 177) reference was made.

Held: (ECJ) The letters were not goods but were services under Art.49 (ex 59). While legislation such as that applicable in the United Kingdom restricted the provision of services, it was justified in the public interest and was not disproportionate. [1994] E.C.R. I-1039

Alpine Investment B.V. v Minister van Financien (Case C-384/93) 1995
Dutch law prohibited "cold calling" (i.e. telephone contact by firms to potential customers without their prior written consent). The restriction applied to all firms established in the Netherlands, regardless of the location of their clients. Alpine Investments, a provider of financial services, was thus unable to canvass potential customers in the United Kingdom.

Held: (ECJ) While such a measure in principle infringed Art.49 (ex 59) it was justified to protect consumers and the Dutch securities market. It was not disproportionate. [1995] E.C.R. I-1141.

Commentary

(1) The ECJ distinguished *Alpine Investments* from *Keck* and *Mithouard*. (See Ch.9.) A restriction on cold calling, unlike legislation on selling arrangements, directly affects access to the market in other Member States and can hinder intra-EC trade.

(2) See also *Säger v Dennenmeyer* (Case C-76/90) in which a United Kingdom company was prevented from exercising patent renewal services in Germany by national legislation. *Held* (ECJ): Although the rules did not discriminate on grounds of nationality, they hindered D's access to the German market and were disproportionate.

(3) In *Laara v Finland* (Case C-124/97) a Finnish national challenged a grant of exclusive rights to operate slot machines, claiming that it infringed Art.49 (ex 59) EC. The ECJ held that, in the light of public interest objectives including the control of gambling, it did not infringe Art.49.

(4) In *Déliege v Ligue Fracophone de Judo* (Joined Cases C-51/96 and C-191/97) the ECJ had to consider Art.49 (ex 59) in the context of participation of individuals known as judokas (professional or semi-professional judo players) in high-level sporting events which do not involve national teams competing with each other. The selection rules of the relevant sporting federations do not contain clauses restricting the number of players by nationality.

　　Once selected, athletes compete on their own account, regardless of nationality. Such rules were found not to infringe Art.49.

Freedom to receive services

Key Principle: **Art.49 (ex 59) covers the freedom to receive as well as to provide services.**

Luisi and Carbone v Ministero del Tesoro (Case 286/83) 1984
Luisi and Carbone had, independently of each other, taken money out of Italy in excess of the amount permitted under exchange control regulations to pay for medical and tourist services. An Art.234 (ex 177) reference was made during their prosecution under Italian law.

Held: (ECJ) Tourists, persons receiving medical treatment and persons travelling for the purpose of education and business are covered by Art.49 (ex 59). [1984] E.C.R. 377.

Commentary

(1) The principle of non-discrimination: Art.12 (ex 6) EC applies to the receipt as well as the provision of services. In *Cowan v Tresor Public* (Case 186/87) a United Kingdom national "mugged" on the Paris Metro, claimed but was refused compensation for his injuries out of public funds. The ECJ held that as a tourist he was entitled to compensation on the basis of equal treatment.

(2) In *Commission v Spain* (Case C-45/93) the ECJ found that charging a discriminatory entrance fee for non-nationals to enter museums infringed Art.12 (ex 6).

(3) The Court of Appeal ruled on the right to receive services in the EU in *R. v Human Fertilisation and Embryology Authority, Ex p. Diane Blood*, following a refusal to allow DB to obtain fertility treatment in another EU state using her dead husband's sperm as he had not given his consent. The CA granted an order in her favour without making a reference to the ECJ, stating that it considered that to have refused would have amounted to an unreasonable restriction on DB's right to travel to receive medical services under Art.49 (ex 59) EC.

(4) The ECJ had to consider the relationship between Art.50 (ex 60) and the receipt of medical services in two recent decisions, *Geraets-Smits v Stichtun Ziekenfonds, Peerbooms v Stichtung CZ Grope Zorgverzekeringen* (Case C-157/99) and *Vanbraekel v Alliance Nationale des Mutualités Chrétiennes* (ANMC) (Case C-368/98). In Geraets-Smits, two applicants were insured for medical costs under an insurance scheme in the Netherlands. Both of the applicants received medical treatment outside the home state without prior authorisation. Funding would only have been approved if the treatment was found to be both "normal" and "necessary". The ECJ (under Art.234) found that these conditions amounted to a restriction on the freedom to provide and receive services. They were, however, capable of objective justification on several grounds, including the interests of maintaining a balanced medical service open to

all. The conditions should be interpreted fairly, in a non-discriminatory manner. Treatment should only be refused on grounds of necessity where the same or equivalent treatment is available without undue delay from an establishment covered by the insurance fund's contractual arrangements.

(5) In *Vanbraekel*, the applicant, a Belgian national had surgery in France despite being refused authorisation from the insurers, ANMC. V sought reimbursement through a tribunal in Belgium, appealing to a higher court when refused. The court ruled that the requirement imposed by the tribunal (certification by a Belgian professor of the need for treatment in France) was excessive.

An expert report ordered by the court found that V required hospital treatment which could be better provided abroad. V died while undergoing surgery in Paris. The action was continued by her heirs. The ECJ (under Art.234) ruled that national legislation which failed to guarantee a person within its social insurance scheme, who had prior authorisation to received hospital treatment in another Member State under Regulation 1408/71, a level of payment equivalent to the rate to which he was entitled in the home state, was contrary to Art.49. The comment of Craig & De Burca *EU Law: Text, Cases and Materials*, 3rd ed., p.810 is significant: [The cases] "undoubtedly open up to the rigours of the Treaty rules and to cross-border economic activity, some of the core aspects of national welfare systems."

The economic element

Key Principle: **"Services" are normally provided for remuneration, in so far as they are not covered by other provisions on free movement of goods, persons and capital: Art.50 (ex 60).**

Society for the Protection of the Unborn Child (Ireland) Ltd v Grogan (Case C-159/90) 1991

Officers of a student association in Ireland (where abortion is illegal) had distributed information without charge about the availability of abortion services in other Member States.

Held: (ECJ) In the absence of an economic element, the provision of information about abortion services in other Member States is outside the scope of Art.49 (ex 59). [1991] E.C.R. 4685.

Commentary

(1) Freedom to move around the EC remains largely dependent on economic status, whether exercising the rights of the worker, of establishment or the provision and receipt of services. Directives have been adopted to provide residence rights for certain categories of individuals who are not economically active: Directive 90/364 (individuals and their families with sickness insurance and sufficient resources), Directive 90/365 (former employees, the self-employed and their families) and Directive 93/96 (students for the duration of their studies).

(2) *Carpenter v Secretary of State for the Home Department* (Case C-60/00) provides an insight into the relationship between Art.49 of the Treaty and Art.8 of the ECHR (respect for family life). The applicant, Mrs C, a national of the Philippines, overstayed her visitor's visa to the UK without permission, marrying a UK national the following year. Mr C ran a business selling space in medical and scientific journals, providing services across the EC. Mrs C appealed to the Immigration Appeals Tribunal (IAT) against a decision to deport her to the Philippines, arguing that she had a right in EC law to remain in the UK. This claim was largely based on Art.49, in relation to indirect support she provided with childcare for Mr C's children. The ECJ (under Art.234) held that Art.49, read in the light of Art.8 of the ECHR (respect for family life) precluded a refusal of the right of residence by the host state to the spouse from a third country of someone providing services in another Member State.

Key Principle: **EU citizens have the right to move and reside freely within the territories of the Member States: Art.18 (ex 8a).**

Kremzow v Austria (Case C-299/95) 1997
K, a retired Austrian judge, was convicted of murder and sentenced to twenty years' imprisonment. His sentence was increased by the appeal court in Austria in 1986 during his absence. The European Court of Human Rights found in 1993 that Art.6 of the ECHR had been breached because he had not

been present to defend himself. K claimed damages against the Austrian Government for unlawful detention in prison and for depriving him of free movement rights under the EC Treaty. The Austrian court made an Art.234 (ex 177) reference to the ECJ.

Held: (ECJ) The matter was outside the scope of EC law, as K had not exercised his free movement rights. A "purely hypothetical prospect" of exercising those rights was insufficient connection with EC law to justify the application of the principles of EC law. [1997] E.C.R. I-2629.

Commentary

(1) Art.17 (ex 8) EC Treaty introduced the category of "citizenship of the Union" for EU nationals, regardless of economic status. Under Art.18 (ex 8a) EU citizens have the right to reside anywhere in the EU, subject to the limitations laid down in the Treaty and in implementation measures.

(2) Kremzow's rights as a European citizen were bound to be hypothetical: prior to his conviction, when K would have been free to travel, Austria was not yet a member of the EU. By the time the concept of European citizenship was introduced, he was in custody.

(3) On European citizenship, see also *Martinez Sala v Freistadt Bayern* (Case C-85/98) in which the ECJ left undecided the question as to whether an individual who is no longer employed or self-employed may enjoy an independent right of residence as an EU national.

(4) The decision in *Bidar* (See Ch.10, p.118) provides support for the concept that economically inactive citizens may nevertheless be able to reply on Art.18, subject to establishing the necessary link. Union citizenship was further developed by the ECJ in *Baumbast v R* (Case C-414/99, in which the ECJ held that Art.18(1) is directly effective. In *Chen and Zhu* (Case C-200/01) the Court recognised the residence rights of the Chinese parents of a child born in Northern Ireland to a mother who then moved to Wales. The parents, seeking to avoid China's 'one child' policy, had originally moved to Northern Ireland for the birth, to enable the child to acquire Irish nationality. The ECJ held that a third country national with sufficient resources who is

the parent or carer of a minor who is an EU national and covered by sickness insurance has indefinite residence rights.

(5) Art.17 EC is implemented by Directive 93/109 (right to vote in EP and local elections). For a decision by the European Court of Human Rights on the question of voting rights, in the EP, see *Matthews*, Ch.3, p.29. In *Commission v Belgium*, the ECJ found that Belgium had infringed Directive 93/109 when it refused to allow nationals other than Belgian nationals to stand and vote in local elections.

(6) Derogation from the principle of free movement is permissible for the non-economically active only under the same terms as for workers and the self-employed under Directive 64/221 (see Ch.10, p.121).

(7) Some relaxation of border controls was in existence before the ToA. Those states which had adopted the Schengen Convention (not the UK, Denmark and Ireland) allowed free movement of EU nationals without passport inspections at borders. This has been incorporated into the EC Treaty as a result of the ToA, subject to an "opt out" by the states not previously participating in Schengen. In *Wijsenbeek* (Case C-387/97), prior to the ToA, the Dutch court sought a preliminary ruling on the question following W's refusal to allow inspection of his passport when travelling from Strasbourg to Rotterdam. The ECJ held that, in the absence of harmonisation measures, Member States remain free to carry out identity checks at borders provided penalties for breach are not disproportionate.

(8) The free movement of persons is also affected by the changes as a result of the ToA, which introduced a new Title IV on Visas, Asylum, Immigration and other policies on the free movement of persons. It is based on an area of security and justice within which the free movement of persons is assured. It was due for implementation by May 1, 2004. The ToA renamed the Third Pillar Provisions on Police and Judicial Co-operation in Criminal Matters. Some areas previously covered by the third pillar have been transferred to the first pillar. The ECJ has increased scope for preliminary rulings in these areas: see Ch.7.

Education and vocational training

Key Principle: **Discrimination in access to vocational training on grounds of nationality infringes Art.12 (ex 6) EC Treaty.**

Gravier v City of Liege (Case 293/83) 1985

Gravier, a French national, had been offered a place by the Academie Royale des Beaux-Arts in Liege on a four year course to study the art of the strip cartoon. She objected to paying the "minerval", an enrolment fee payable by students who were not Belgian nationals, claiming that the payment infringed Art.12 (ex 6, but then 7 of the EEC Treaty) and Art.49 (ex 59) (receipt of services). An Art.234 (ex 177) reference was made.

Held: (ECJ) (1) Conditions of access to vocational training are covered by the Treaty. The imposition of a fee such as the "minerval" on students who are not nationals of the host state constitutes discrimination contrary to Art.7.

(2) Any form of education which prepares for a qualification orparticular profession, trade or employment, or which provides the necessary training and skills for such a profession, trade or employment is vocational training, even if the programme includes an element of general education. [1985] E.C.R. 593.

Commentary

(1) Note that the principle of non-discrimination now in Art.12 was originally numbered Art.7 in the Treaty of Rome, the provision being renumbered Art.6 by the SEA. As an example of the application of the principle in Art.12 (ex 6) see *Bickel* and *Franz* (Case C-274/96) in which the ECJ held that the right to have criminal proceedings conducted in a language other than the principal language of the state concerned was covered by the principle of non-discrimination in Art.12. A national rule providing for such an entitlement which was not extended to the residents of other areas infringed Art.12 (ex 6).

(2) The ECJ has interpreted "vocational training" widely, to cover almost all undergraduate degrees except those intended to benefit general knowledge rather than to prepare for a profession: *Barra v Belgium and City of Liege* (Case 309/85). In *Blaizot v University of Liege* (Case 24/86) the ECJ held that a six year veterinary course, the first half of which was academic and the second half vocational, should be regarded as a single course of vocational training. The consequence of *Gravier* and subsequent decisions has been that EC nationals attending undergraduate degree

courses in EC states other than their own can no longer be charged higher fees than home students. There is no entitlement to a grant from the host state: *Brown v Secretary of State for Scotland* (Case 197/86) and *Lair v University of Hanover* (Case 39/86). But see *Bidar* (Case C-209/03) (p.118).

12. COMPETITION LAW 1

Agreements and restrictive practices under Article 81

The prohibition

Key Principle: The following are prohibited as incompatible with the common market: all agreements between undertakings, decisions by associations of undertakings and concerted practices which may affect trade between Member States, and which have as their object or effect the prevention, restriction or distortion of competition within the common market: Art.81(1) (ex 85(1)).

Agreements between undertakings

Key Principle: Agreements between undertakings are prohibited.

ACF Chemiefarma v Commission (Case 41/69) 1970
Quinine producers entered into an export agreement relating to trade with third countries and a "gentlemen's agreement" in 1962 governing the conduct of its members in the common market. In the export agreement the parties agreed to be bound by the gentlemen's agreement. The Commission found that both agreements were an indivisible entity and contravened Art.81 (ex 85). The applicants challenged the decision in the ECJ under Art.230 (ex 173).

Held: (ECJ) Having regard to the conduct of the parties in relation to sharing domestic markets, the fixing of common prices, determination of sales quotas and prohibition of making synthetic quinine, it was clear that the parties intended to be bound by the gentlemen's agreement which amounted to a restriction on competition contrary to Art.81 (ex 85). [1970] E.C.R. 661.

Commentary

(1) An agreement may be caught by Art.81 even where it is nota legally binding contract. The ACF Chemiefarma (Quinine Producers) gentlemen's agreement was covered because it

could be enforced through arbitration. The agreement is an example of a horizontal agreement, which seeks to partition the EC on national lines.

(2) An individual undertaking involved in a cartel may be held responsible for the overall cartel where the Commission can demonstrate that, during a given period, each undertaking consented to the adoption of an overall plan comprising the constituent elements of a cartel or that it participated directly in all these elements during the period: *Buchman*, etc. (Cases T-295/94, etc.) ("Cartonboard").

(3) Any legal or natural person engaged in economic activity may be regarded as an undertaking, e.g. an opera singer in *Re Unitel* (Commission Decision, 1978).

(4) The competition rules in Arts 81 and 82 are extended to public undertakings engaging in commercial activity by Art.86 (ex 90): *Italy v Sacchi* (Case 155/73).

(5) Agreements between parent companies and subsidiaries are not regarded as agreements between undertakings where they form a single economic unit: *Viho Europe BV v Commission* (Case T-102/92).

(6) Decisions by associations usually involve trade associations, often acting informally. Such decisions may breach Art.81 (ex 85).

Concerted practices

Key Principle: **A concerted practice arises where positive steps short of an agreement have been taken to align the activities of undertakings.**

Imperial Chemical Industries Ltd v Commission ("Dyestuffs") (Case 48/69) 1972
ICI was one of 10 undertakings, which together produced about 80 per cent of the market in dyestuffs in the EC. It was the first undertaking to announce a price rise in 1964, shortly followed by identical increases by the other dyestuff producers. Further increases took place in 1965 and 1967, again mirrored by the other producers. The Commission decided that there had been a concerted practice contrary to Art.81 (ex 85) and imposed fines on the undertakings. The undertakings challenged the decision

under Art.230 (ex 173) in the ECJ, claiming that the price rises had not resulted from a concerted practice but from parallel behaviour in an oligopolistic market (i.e. in a market dominated by a few producers, with each producer following the "priceleader").

Held: (ECJ) (1) From the number of producers concerned, it could not be said that the European dyestuffs market operated on the basis of oligopoly (dominance by a few producers). Price competition should have continued to operate, making it inconceivable that parallel pricing would occur.

(2) The general and uniform increase on the various markets could only have arisen as a result of a common intention by the undertakings to adjust prices and to avoid the risks of competition. [1972] E.C.R. 619.

Commentary

(1) It is necessary to examine price rises, even where they are identical or very similar, to decide whether they reflect an independent response to the market or evidence of a concerted practice. The ECJ in "*Dyestuffs*" considered that the producers had eliminated uncertainty between themselves over future behaviour and, therefore, most of the risk inherent in independent change of conduct.

(2) The ECJ limited its stance on behaviour amounting to a concerted practice in *Ahlström oy v Commission ("Wood-pulp")* (Joined Cases C-89, etc. /85), a decision arising out of the practice of woodpulp producers of announcing maximum price rises on a quarterly basis to their customers. The ECJ found no breach of Art.81 (ex 85), holding (on the facts) that the price announcements to users constituted market behaviour which did not lessen each undertaking's uncertainty as to the future attitude of its competitors.

Effect on inter-member trade

Key Principle: **There must be an effect on inter-member trade.**

Societe Technique Miniere v Maschinenbau Ulm GmbH (Case 56/65) 1966

MBU agreed to give STM exclusive distribution rights in France of heavy earth-moving equipment on condition that STM would not sell competing machines. The agreement was challenged before a French court, which made an Art.234 (ex 177) reference to the ECJ.

Held: (ECJ) "It must be possible to foresee ... that the agreement in question may have an influence, direct or indirect, actual or potential, on the pattern of trade between Member States". [1966] E.C.R. 235.

Commentary

(1) The ruling demonstrates the wide interpretation placed by the ECJ in *STM v Maschinenbau* on "effect on trade between Member States". It means that an agreement will be covered by the prohibition even where it relates to a single Member State, provided there is a potential for exports to another Member State. See e.g. *Pronuptia v Schillgalis* (Case 161/84) in which a franchising agreement intended to relate to a territory within Germany was found to have a potential effect on trade.

(2) A very different (potentially positive) effect on trade may be seen in *Publishers Association v Commission* (Case C-360/92P) where the ECJ overturned part of the CFI's decision to refuse exemption to the Net Book Agreements (a series of agreements between book publishers and retailers providing for certain books to be sold at fixed prices). The basis for the ECJ decision was that the CFI had failed to take proper account of the benefits to the book trade from the single language area formed by the British and Irish book markets. Soon after the ECJ decision, the Net Book Agreements collapsed due to commercial pressures.

Prevention, restriction or distortion of competition

Key Principle: **An agreement is prohibited if its object or effect is to prevent, restrict or distort competition.**

Consten and Grundig v Commission (Joined Cases 56 & 58/64) 1966

The German electronics company G entered into an exclusive distribution agreement with C whereby G agreed to supply C as sole distributor in France. In return C agreed not to sell any competing products in France or to re-export Grundig products. In addition, C was granted sole use in France of G's international trade mark (GINT). UNEF, another French company, bought Grundig products in Germany where they were sold more cheaply and resold them in France. C sued UNEF in the French courts for infringement of the GINT trade mark. UNEF applied successfully to the Commission for a decision that the agreement between G and C infringed Art.81 (ex 85). G and C challenged the decision in the ECJ under Art.230 (ex 173).

Held: (ECJ) (1) The object of the distribution agreement was to eliminate competition to the detriment of consumers.

(2) There is no need to take account of the effects of an agreement once it appears that it has as its object the prevention, restriction or distortion of competition. [1966] E.C.R. 299.

Commentary

(1) The use of the GINT trade mark could not be enforced by *Consten* because it had the effect of partitioning the market along national lines.

(2) The ECJ decided that the list of illegal practices set out after the prohibition in Art.81(1) (ex 85(1)) is illustrative rather than exhaustive. The practices include agreements to fix prices, limit production or markets, apply different conditions to equivalent transactions and impose unconnected supplementary obligation.

(3) The decision in *Consten* and *Grundig* has been criticised because it prohibits vertical agreements (i.e. agreements between undertakings at different levels of distribution, in this case between producer and distributor). Vertical agreements are seen as less damaging to consumers than horizontal agreements (i.e. agreements between undertakings at the same level of distribution, such as a cartel between retailers). Some commentators have thus taken the view that it is not necessary to ban agreements which restrict the availability of a particular brand where there is effective inter-brand competition (i.e. competition between brands).

Key Principle: **It is not necessary to carry out a market analysis where the object of the agreement is to prevent, restrict or distort competition.**

Societe Technique Miniere v Maschinenbau (Case 56/65) 1966
For facts, see p.128.

Held: (ECJ) (1) The terms "object or effect" are "disjunctive" (i.e. alternatives). (2) Exclusive distribution agreements do not necessarily restrict competition. [1966] E.C.R. 235.

Commentary

(1) Where it is not apparent that the object of the agreement is to restrict competition, a market analysis should be carried out to determine whether the effects of the agreement infringe Art.81(1)(ex 85(1)).

(2) The following factors were identified in STM as relevant for consideration in a market analysis: (a) the market shares of the parties; (b) whether the agreement formed part of a network; (c) the nature or quantity of the products to which the agreement relates; (d) the severity of the restrictions; and (e) whether parallel imports or re-exports were prohibited.

Key Principle: **A distribution agreement will infringe Art.85(1) where it substantially excludes other dealers.**

Delimitis v Henninger Vrau (Case C-234/89) 1991
A tenant challenged the requirement under a beer supply agreement to buy all the beer for his bar from his landlord, claiming that it infringed Art.81(1) (ex 85(1)). An Art.234 (ex 177) reference was made.

Held: (ECJ) (1) A full analysis was needed to establish whether so many outlets were tied to brewers that there were insufficient independent outlets to provide a viable market for a new brewer to supply. (2) A selective distribution system does not infringe Art.81(1) (ex 85(1)) where resellers are chosen on the basis of objective criteria of a qualitative nature and the conditions for the application of such criteria are laid down for all potential resellers. [1991] E.C.R. I-935.

Commentary

(1) Delimitis repeats the formula previously adopted by the ECJ in *Metro-Grossmarkte GmbH v Commission* (Case 326/76) in relation to selective distribution systems. The approach of the ECJ reflects the concept, borrowed from the United States' antitrust law, known as the "rule of reason". Applying the rule of reason, agreements that are not automatically illegal are considered within the context of the market to decide whether they are anti-competitive. Article 81(3) (ex 85(3)) recognises this pragmatic approach by providing for exemption from the consequences of illegality under Art.81(2) (ex 85(2)): see p.138 below. Negative clearance may be granted by the Commission where the agreement does not infringe Art.81(1) though this system will change when power is devolved to the national authorities under Regulation 1/2003 (see below).

(2) Other examples of a "rule of reason" approach include: (a) *Remia and Nutricia v Commission* (Case 42/84): restrictive terms in the sale of a business did not infringe Art.85(1) if necessary to give effect to the sale; and (b) *Pronuptia v Schillgallis* (Case 161/84): restrictive clauses in franchise agreements did not breach Art.81(1) if necessary to ensure the identity of the franchiser's network or to prevent know-how being transferred to competitors.

(3) In *Courage v Creehan* (Case C-453/99) the ECJ laid down important principles on the right of an individual under Art.81 to pursue a remedy in the national courts, holding that a party to a contract liable to restrict or distort competition under Art.81 can rely on the breach of that provision to obtain relief from the other party to the contract. The Court also ruled that Art.81 precludes a rule of national law under which a party to a contract which is illegal under Art.81 is barred for claiming damages for loss caused by performance of that contract solely because the claimant is a party to that contract, unless the party claiming bears significant responsibility for the breach of Art.81.

Within the common market

Key Principle: **Anti-competitive agreements are covered by Art.81(1) if they are between undertakings situated within the**

EC or between undertakings situated outside the EC, where the effects of the agreement are felt within the EC.

ICI v Commission ("Dyestuffs") (Case 48/69) 1972

For facts, see p.127. Several of the undertakings engaged in concerted practices over price increases were based outside the EC, in Switzerland and in the United Kingdom (prior to membership).

Held: (ECJ) Because the effects of their practices were felt within the EC, the undertakings were liable for breaches of Art.81(1) (ex 85(1)). The United Kingdom parent company, ICI (UK) Ltd, was liable for the breaches of its Dutch subsidiary.

Commentary

(1) *Dyestuffs* does not represent an entirely clear statement about the "effects" doctrine, since the issues were addressed mainly in terms of liability for the acts of subsidiaries.

(2) In *Ahlström Osakeyhito v Commission ("Wood Pulp")* (Joined Cases 89, etc./85) (see p.128) forestry undertakings in Finland, Sweden and Canada (all, at that time, outside the EC) challenged the Commission decision that their advance notification of price rises infringed Art.85. The ECJ held that there was a breach of Art.81 (ex 85) because the practices were implemented within the EC. It was immaterial whether they had used subsidiaries, agents or branches within the Member States.

Minor agreements

Key Principle: **Agreements producing a negligible effect on trade do not infringe Art.81(1).**

Völk v Vervaecke (Case 5/69)

Völk, a producer of washing machines with about 0.2 to 0.5 per cent of the market in Germany and an even smaller market share in Belgium and Luxembourg, entered on agreement with Vervaecke. Under the agreement Vervaecke, a Dutch distributor of electrical products, was given exclusive rights to distribute Völk's products in Belgium and Luxembourg, with a further ban on parallel imports.

Held: (ECJ) There was no appreciable effect on competition and therefore no breach of Art.81(1) (ex 85(1)). [1969] E.C.R. 295.

Commentary
The Commission has adopted a series of Notices on Minor Agreements. As Notices are non-binding, they may only be taken as indicative of the Commission's position. The most recent Notice was issued in 2001. It provides that agreements between undertakings concerned with production or distribution do not infringe.

Art.81(1) where the market share of the undertakings does not exceed 10 per cent (for agreements between competitors) and 15 per cent (for agreement between non-competitors). A 10 per cent threshold applies to agreements which are difficult to classify according to these categories.

Illegality and exemption

Key Principle: **Any agreements or decisions prohibited under Art.81(1) are automatically void: Art.81(2).**

Consten and Grundig v Commission (Joined Cases 56 & 58/64) 1966
For facts, see p.129.

Held: (ECJ) Only the parts of the agreement which restricted competition were void (i.e. those relating to restrictions on parallel importation of goods).

Commentary

(1) The decision in *Consten* and *Grundig* illustrates that the application of Art.81(2) (ex 85(2)) need not lead to the invalidity of the entire agreement (contrary to the earlier decision by the Commission).

(2) Before May 1, 2004 the prohibition under Art.81(1) could be declared inapplicable by the Commission where two positive and two negative conditions are satisfied under Regulation 17/62 (as amended). The agreement must contribute to improving production or distribution of goods, or to promoting technical or economic progress.

(3) A New approach to ex-exemption was introduced on May 1, 2004 when Regulation 1/2003 came into effect. Under the Regulation, much of the power currently held by the

Commission devolved to the national competition authorities (NCAs), leaving the Commission free to concentrate on
significant cases raising new issues. Notification to the
Commission, was abolished. The Regulation implements the
1999 White Paper on Modernisation which proposed extensive changes to the system of competition enforcement.
Devolution to the national authorities was needed in order
to deal with the volume of applications which exceeded the
capacity of the Commission to respond.

(4) Under Art.1 of Regulation 1/2003 agreements caught by
Art.81(1) which do not satisfy Art.81(3) are prohibited, no
prior decision to that effect being required. Art.2 makes
similar provision in relation to infringements of Art.82.
Parties should make their own assessments as to whether the
agreement complies with EC competition law. The Commission is, however, empowered under Art.4(2) of the Regulation to adopt regulations requiring registration in relation
to certain types of agreement caught by Art.81(1). Registration will not provide any legal rights.

Key Principle: **The agreement must not impose any restrictions that are not indispensable.**

Consten and Grundig v Commission (Joined Cases 56 & 58/64)
For facts, see p.129.

Held: (ECJ) The use of the GINT trademark in France was not
required by the agreement. That part of the agreement was void.

Commentary
It is possible to sever an illegal part of an agreement where the rest
is valid.

Key Principle: **There must be no elimination of competition.**

**Metropole Television SA (M6) v Commission (Joined Cases
T-185/00, T-216/00 and T-300/00)**
The CFI considered a complaint arising out of a Commission
decision granting exemption to a set of rules adopted by the

European Broadcasting Union for the granting of sub-licences to third parties for broadcasting rights to sporting events. The applicants were various television companies denied licences under the EBU rules. The Court confirmed the existence of an "upstream" market for the acquisition of rights and a "downstream" market for the televised transmission of sporting events. Television rights are normally granted on a territorial, exclusive basis. CFI found that the sub-licensing system did not guarantee the applicants, competitors of the members of the EBU, sufficient access to transmission rights for sporting events.

HELD: (CFI) The Commission was wrong to decide that the sub-licensing scheme guaranteed access for third parties, avoiding the elimination of competition, even if a product market limited to certain major sporting events exists.

Key Principle: **Comfort letters are not legally binding.**

Lancôme v ETOS (Case 99/79) 1980

The parties had notified a selective distribution system for perfumes to the Commission under Regulation 17/62. While no formal decision had been issued, a "comfort letter" had been received stating that the system was not regarded as breaching Art.81(1) (ex 85(1)). A number of retailers whom the perfume manufacturers had refused to supply challenged the system under Art.81(1) (ex 85(1)a) in the French courts. An Art.234 (ex 177) reference was made.

Held: (ECJ) (1) Comfort letters are administrative letters outside the structure of the Treaty; they do not bind national courts and cannot be regarded as decisions capable of annulment under Art.230 (ex 173). (2) Such agreements may infringe Art.81(1) (ex 85(1)) where the test for admission to the selective distribution system is quantitative rather than qualitative (i.e. based on limiting the number of dealers rather than on objective criteria). [1980] E.C.R. 2511.

Commentary

(1) The Commission issued a number of block (or group) exemptions to cover commonly occurring commercial practices. Where an agreement is covered by a block exemption

there is no need to notify the NCA as the agreement has full validity under Art.81(3) (ex 85(3)). Block exemption regulations were issued in areas including exclusive distribution, exclusive purchasing, research and development, specialisation, franchising and technology transfer. Most specify maximum turnover limits. If the undertakings' turnover exceeds the limit, it is not covered by the block exemption and will require an individual exemption to ensure validity. New block exemption agreements were adopted between 1996 and 2000, mostly for a 10 year period.

(2) New vertical agreements will be covered by the block exemption on vertical agreements, Regulation 270/99, adopted in December 1999, to run for 10 years from June 1, 2000. Vertical agreements are defined as "agreements or concerted practices entered into between two or more undertakings, each of whom operates, for the purpose of the agreement, at a different level of production or distribution chain, and relating to the conditions under which the parties may purchase, sell or resell certain goods or services." The regulation specifies threshold limits (30 per cent of the relevant market), above which notification will be necessary. Certain restraints such as resale price maintenance restrictions on resales and restrictions to users in selective distribution agreements are not covered. Vertical agreements covered by other block exemptions are affected by the regulations.

(3) The UK passed the Competition Act in 1998, introducing anew regime for the administration of national competition rules based on Arts 81 and 82 EC, to be enforced mainly by the Director General of Fair Trading. Under the Act the UK competition authorities must ensure consistency with the principles of the EC Treaty, the case law of the European Courts and the decisions and statements of the Commission.

13. COMPETITION LAW 2

Abuse of a dominant position under Article 82

Key Principle: Any abuse by one or more undertakings of a dominant position within the common market or in a substantial part of it shall be prohibited under Art.82 (ex 86) as incompatible with the common market in so far as it may affect trade between Member States.

Dominance

Key Principle: Dominance results from a position of economic strength, which enables an undertaking to act independently of its competitors and consumers.

Hoffman-La Roche v Commission ("Vitamins") (Case 85/76) 1979
H-LR held the following market shares in relation to vitamins: A—47 per cent; B2—86 per cent; B3—64 per cent; B6–95 per cent; C—68 per cent; E—70 per cent and H—95 per cent, with 65 per cent of the worldwide market for vitamins in 1974.

Held: (ECJ) (1) H-LR could be presumed to be dominant in all vitamin markets except Vitamin A. Dominance could be shown in relation to A, as H-LR held substantially more of the market than the nearest competitor.

(2) "The existence of a dominant position may derive from several factors which, taken separately, are not necessarily determinative but among those factors a highly important one is the existence of a very large market share". [1979] E.C.R. 461.

Commentary

(1) Size and turnover alone do not establish dominance. Other relevant factors identified by the ECJ include the absence of a significant competitor and the extent to which the sales network is developed.

(2) As the case law of the ECJ developed it became clear that dominance is a legal rather than an exclusively economic policy. It is established by carrying out an analysis of the relevant product, geographical and (where appropriate) temporal or seasonal markets.

(3) Note that to prove a breach of Art.82, it is not enough merely to establish dominance. There must also be abuse of a dominant position.

The product market

Key Principle: **It is essential to identify the product market correctly before a breach of Art.82 may be established.**

Europemballage Corporation and Continental Can Co Inc v Commission ("Continental Can") (Case 6/72) 1975
Continental Can Co Inc (CC) were major producers of metal packages. In 1969 they took over a German company, Schmalbach (S). In 1970 CC agreed through its subsidiary, Europemballage, to acquire a majority holding in a Dutch company, Thomassen (T). At the time of the takeover of T, S and T were not in competition, although they were operating in adjacent geographical areas and were both making metal packaging. The Commission investigated the takeover of T, responsibility for which was imputed to CC by the enterprise entity concept (see Ch.12, p.143: *Viho Europe*). The Commission decided that CC, through its holding in S, was dominant on the market for metal packaging for fish and meat and for metal closures for glass containers. It also found that the purchase of T amounted to an abuse of that position. CC and E challenged the decision under Art.230 (ex 173).

Held: (ECJ) The Commission had failed to identify the relevant product market and had not given reasons for its decision. The decision was annulled. [1975] E.C.R. 495.

Commentary

(1) While agreeing in principle that a takeover such as CC sacquisition of T could be a breach of Art.82 (ex 86), the ECJ in *Continental Can* made it clear that the Commission's failure to take sufficient account of the relevant product

market was a ground for annulment. The Commission should have analysed the undertaking's market power by defining the relevant market and then assessing the extent of dominance within that market. While there had been some consideration of possible substitutes on the demand side (meat and fish suppliers using plastic containers) it had not considered substitutes on the supply side (packaging manufacturers making alternative containers).

(2) Two key factors may be identified when identifying the product market: cross-elasticity of demand and cross-elasticity of supply (availability of demand/supply substitutes).

(3) Korah (in EC Competition Law and Practice, 7th ed., p.83) points out that the Commission's approach in *Continental Can* follows the practice of using a test based on demand substitution to define the market. (The test entails considering which undertaking is accused, which products are involved, who are the customers and what alternatives are open to those customers.) In recent judgments the ECJ has focused more closely on crosselasticity of substitutes on both the supply and demand sides, as in its judgment in *Continental Can*.

Key Principle: **The product market should be defined by reference to product substitution, i.e. whether it is possible to interchange another product regarded by customers as identical.**

United Brands v Commission (Case 22/76) 1978

The Commission issued a decision that United Brands had infringed Art.82 (ex 86) in the marketing of bananas grown by themselves in the EC. It considered that there was a separate market for bananas, which were not interchangeable with other fruit. United Brands challenged the decision in the ECJ on the basis that it did not hold a dominant position in the market, claiming that the relevant product market was fresh fruit and not bananas.

Held: (ECJ) The banana has special characteristics (e.g. taste, softness, ease of handling) which make it very suitable for the very young, old and sick. There is little substitutability between bananas and other fruit. The banana market is a distinct market, separate from other fruits. [1978] E.C.R. 207.

Commentary

(1) The product market defined in United Brands was fairly narrow and related to substitutability from the demand side. An even more limited product market was identified in *Hugin-Kassaregister A.B. v Commission* (Case 22/78): spare parts to repair cash registers made by Hugin. See also *Hoffman-La Roche* (Case 85/76) (see p.154), in which each vitamin was found to occupy an individual product market. In some cases, it is the possibility of substitution from the supply side which is relevant. In *Tetra-Pak Rausing S.A. v Commission* (Case T-51/89), upheld by the ECJ in Case C-333/94P, the CFI held that the makers of milk packaging machines could not readily transfer to making aseptic packaging for UHT milk, justifying the finding that aseptic packaging was a distinct product market.

(2) In 1997 the Commission issued the Notice on Market Definition. This defined the relevant product market as "all those products and/or services which are regarded as interchangeable by the consumer, by reason of the products' characteristics, their prices and their intended uses". The Notice puts the question as to whether the parties' customers would switch to readily available substitutes or to suppliers located elsewhere in the event of a hypothetical but permanent price increase (5–10 per cent) in the product and areas considered.

The geographical market

Key Principle: **It is necessary to show that dominance occurs within the common market or a substantial part of it.**

Michelin (N.V. Nederlandsche Baden-industrie Michelin) v Commission (Case 322/81) 1983

The Commission found that there was an abuse of a dominant position arising out of the practices of the Dutch subsidiary of Michelin in the Netherlands. The Michelin group operated a policy of price discounts which made it difficult for their customers to obtain tyres for heavy vehicles from manufacturers competing with Michelin. The product market was identified by the Commission as tyres for heavy vehicles and the geographical market as the Netherlands, where the activities of the subsidiary were concentrated.

Held: (ECJ) The Commission decision on the product and geographical markets was upheld and the abuse confirmed. [1983] E.C.R. 3461.

Commentary

(1) The geographical market may be, but is not always, the same as the sales area of the undertaking concerned. Where the product is readily transportable (in this case, nail cartridges) it may be the whole of the EC: *Hilti v Commission* (Case T-30/89). Some products may have a global market: *"Wood Pulp"*. The territories of most of the Member States have been found to be a substantial part of the common market (e.g. Ireland in *RTE, BBC and ITP v Commission* (Case C-241/91P)). The ECJ was prepared to define the geographical market very narrowly in *Corsica Ferries v Corpo dei Piloti del Porto di Genoa* (Case C-18/93) as the Port of Genoa.

(2) It is rarely necessary to define the seasonal or temporal market. The ECJ considered seasonal factors in *United Brands* (Case 22/76) but decided that they did not influence consumer choice to a significant degree. Temporal factors were considered but rejected in *Michelin* (Case 322/81). Issues such as the need to build a new factory or for customers to assess the suitability of a new type of tyre were held to be too long term to affect competition.

(3) The 1997 Notice on Market Definition defines the relevant geographical market as "the area in which the undertakings concerned are involved in the supply and demand for products and services, in which the conditions of competition are sufficiently homogenous and which can be distinguished from neighbouring areas because the conditions of competition are appreciably different in those areas".

Assessing dominance

Key Principle: **A detailed market analysis is needed to assess dominance, taking account of the market share of the undertaking and of competitors, control of production and distribution, and financial and technical resources.**

United Brands (Case 22/76) 1978
For facts and decision, see p.156.

Commentary
Market share should be examined carefully in relation to competitors. Although the market share of *United Brands* was fairly low (about 40 per cent), the market was fragmented, with no competitor holding more than 16 per cent. United Brands was also identified by the ECJ as possessing superior technology to its competitors. United Brands controlled virtually all stages of production and distribution, owning the banana plantations, and controlling transportation, distribution and ripening of its brand "Chiquita". Taking all these factors into account, it was clear that United Brands was in a dominant position in the banana market in the EC.

Abuse of a dominant position

Key Principle: **Dominance is not illegal. Article 82 is only infringed where a dominant position is abused.**

Key Principle: **Abuse may be demonstrated by practices such as charging unfair prices, discriminating between customers and refusing to supply customers.**

United Brands v Commission (Case 22/76) 1978
United Brands had engaged in a range of practices that the Commission had decided were abusive; including forbidding the sale of green bananas, refusing to supply a Danish wholesaler because it had engaged in an advertising campaign for a competitor (thus driving it out of business), charging customers in different Member States different prices and charging excessive prices. United Brands challenged the findings of abuse in the ECJ.

Held: (ECJ) United Brands had engaged in abuse in relation to the ban on the sale of green bananas, the refusal to supply the Danish wholesaler and differential pricing. Abuse was not proved in relation to alleged excessive pricing.

Commentary

(1) The prohibition in Art.82 is followed by a list of examples of abuse similar to those in Art.81 (ex 85) (imposing unfair prices or other trading conditions, limiting production, markets or technical development to the detriment of consumers, applying dissimilar conditions to equivalent transactions and imposing unnecessarily supplementary obligations). The *United Brands* decision provides examples of most types.

(2) The ECJ and various academic commentators have divided abuses into exploitative abuses (taking advantage of a dominant position by imposing harsh trading conditions such as charging differential prices) and anti-competitive abuses (activities which are not necessarily unfair but which may reduce competition such as mergers: see below). Many examples of abuse show characteristics of both types.

(3) Another example of tying can be seen in *Van Den Bergh Foods Ltd v Commission* (Case T-65/98). Here, Van Den Bergh Foods Ltd, formerly HB Ice Cream Ltd (HB) a manufacturer of ice cream, supplied retailers with freezer cabinets either free or at a nominal charge on condition that the freezers were used exclusively for HB products. The relevant product market was single wrapped impulse ice cream. At least 40 per cent of the retails outlets of this type of ice cream had freezers supplied by HB under its exclusivity agreements. The CFI found that the HB arrangements constituted tying and were an abuse.

   The practices of the company restricted commercial freedom of choice of retailers of ice cream in relation to the products which they stocked.

(4) An example of a practice which may be abusive (both exploitative and anti-competitive) is the granting of discounts. In *Hoffman-La Roche* the ECJ distinguished between loyalty and quantity discounts. Loyalty discounts were granted to customers on the proportion of the customer's requirement for vitamins purchased. This had a "tying"

effect, compelling customers to buy from H-LR and was abusive. Quantity discounts were granted on the basis of volume of vitamins bought from the same firm and were legal.

(5) Export and import bans are usually considered to be abusive: *BMW Belgium v Commission* (Joined Cases 32, etc./78) (export ban considered abusive even though there was national price control leading to particularly low prices in the country of export).

Further examples of abuse

Key Principle: **It is an abuse of a dominant position to refuse to supply a customer.**

RTE, BBC and ITP v Commission (Case C-241/91 P) 1995
RTE, the BBC and the ITP refused to supply Magill, a publisher in Ireland, with information about weekly television listings for the purpose of producing an independent guide. The Commission and CFI found that the refusal was an abuse of a dominant position. A further challenge was brought by the television companies in the ECJ.

Held: (ECJ) The ECJ accepted that weekly television listings amounted to a distinct market in which the television companies were dominant. The companies could not rely on intellectual property rights to justify refusal to supply the information, such refusal amounting to an abuse. [1995] E.C.R. I-743.

Commentary

(1) See also *Commercial Solvents* (Joined Cases 6 & 7/73) in which a dominant undertaking refused to supply a former competitor with an essential chemical, driving it out of business. This was held by the ECJ to be abusive.

(2) Another case involving refusal to supply was *Microsoft Corporation v Commission* (on appeal Case T-201/04) The Commission found that Microsoft's refusal to supply 'inter-operability information' to customers was an abuse. In addition, Microsoft was found to have required any customer acquiring the 'Windows PC operating system' also to buy Windows Media Player, a form of tying. The decision is currently subject to appeal to the CFI.

(3) Refusal to supply was also at the heart of the Court's decision in *IMS Health* (Case C-418/01). The case arose in the context of a dispute between two companies specialising in market analysis of pharmaceutical products and health care. One of the companies that it was entitled to use a 'brick structure' (a system for storing data on pharmaceutical products) developed by the other company, which refused to grant a licence to use the structure. On a referral under Art.234 from the German court, the ECJ found that, in order to decide whether the refusal of a licence was abusive, it should consider the degree of participation by users in developing the system, particularly in terms of cost. A refusal to grant a licence could be abusive where the applicant for the licence intends to offer new products or services on the supply of data in question for which there is a potential consumer demand, the refusal is not justified by objective considerations and the effect of the refusal will be to eliminate all competition in the relevant market.

Key Principle: **"Predatory" pricing is an abuse under Art.82.**

AKZO *Chemie v Commission* **(Case C-62/86) 1991**
ECS, a small undertaking in the United Kingdom producing benzyl peroxide, supplied its product to customers for use as bleach in flour refining. In 1979 it decided to widen its market and sell to users in the polymer industry. AKZO, a Dutch undertaking dominant in polymers, told ECS that it would lower its prices in the flour additive market to a level with which ECS could not compete. AKZO duly reduced its prices. The Commission found that AKZO's price reduction was "predatory" and imposed an exemplary fine. The Commission took account not only of the cost in comparison to the price, but also whether it was part of a strategy to eliminate competition, what the effects of the price reduction would be and the likely reaction of the competitor. AKZO appealed to the ECJ.

Held: (ECJ) (1) The Commission's finding under Art.82 (ex 86) was upheld: AKZO's behaviour amounted to predatory pricing and was an abuse of a dominant position.

(2) Prices below average variable cost give rise to a presumption of predatory pricing. [1986] 3 C.M.L.R. 273.

(3) The amount of the fine was reduced. [1991] E.C.R. I-3359.

Commentary
While price competition usually benefits the consumer, predatory pricing does not. Its aim is to drive the competitor out of business, thus reducing consumer choice. The reasoning of the ECJ in AKZO was followed by the ECJ in *Tetra Pak International v Commission* (Case C-333/94P) where Tetra Pak's pricing of non-aseptic cartons was found to be predatory.

Mergers and concentrations

Key Principle: **Mergers and takeovers may be an abuse of a dominant position under Art.82.**

Europemballage and Continental Can v Commission **(Case 6/72) 1973**
For facts and decision, see p.155.

Commentary

(1) Although the ECJ annulled the Commission's decision that the takeover of Thomassen by Europemballage was an abuse of a dominant position under Art.82 (ex 86) (due to inadequate definition of the market and failure to give reasons), it established in principle that Art.82 may be invoked to control mergers and takeovers.

(2) Art.82 does not provide any mechanism for notification comparable to notification under Art.81(3), making it difficult for undertakings engaged in a merger to protect themselves in the event of a merger being considered abusive. In *BAT & Reynolds v Commission* (Joined Cases 142 & 156/84) the ECJ raised the possibility of mergers being subject to Art.81 (ex 85). This decision opened up the possibility of adopting the Merger Regulation (see below) which provided for advance notification of mergers.

Control of concentrations

Key Principle: **"Concentrations" (as joint ventures such as mergers and takeovers are known under the Regulation) must** be notified to the Commission if they have a community dimension and satisfy specified turnover limits: Regulation 139/2004.

Key Principle: Factors to be considered by the Commission in deciding whether to clear a concentration include the structure of the markets, the market position of the parties, competition inside and outside the EC, barriers to entry, technical and economic progress and the interests of consumers.

Aerospatiale/ Alexia/ De Havilland 1991

Aerospatiale, a French undertaking, and Alenia, an Italian undertaking, agreed to take over from Boeing the assets of the Canadian division of De Havilland. The proposed concentration was notified to the Commission.

Held: (Commission) Clearance under Regulation 4064/89 was refused on the basis that the move would create a new undertaking with an overwhelmingly powerful position in the market for commuter aircraft (holding 50 per cent of the world market and 67 per cent of the EC market). The Commission's analysis found that the merger would be likely to have the following consequences: (a) to increase the new undertaking's market share without leading to economies of scale; (b) to cause the withdrawal of some competitors from the market; and (c) to create barriers to entry for potential competitors. [1992] 4 C.M.L.R. M.2.

Commentary

(1) *Aerospatiale* is an early example of a merger being refused clearance under Regulation 4064/89. This Regulation has now been amended and recast by Regulation 139/2004;

(2) Concentrations are covered by Regulation 139/2004 where the undertakings concerned:

- have a combined aggregate worldwide turnover of at least €5 thousand million;
- the EC-wide turnover of at least two of the undertakings exceeds €100 million;

- the combined aggregate worldwide turnover of all the undertakings concerned is more than €25 million:
- in each of at least three Member States, the combined turnover of all undertakings concerned exceeds €100 million;
- in each of the three Member States (where relevant) the turnover of at least two exceeds €25 million;
- The aggregate EC-wide turnover of at least two of the undertakings concerned is more than €25 million, unless each of the undertakings concerned achieves more than two thirds of its aggregate EC-wide turnover in one and the same Member State.

Concentrations that are not cleared are illegal; undertakings responsible for them are to be fined.

(3) In *Gencor v Commission* (Case T-102/96) the CFI ruled that Regulation 4064/89 applies to collective dominant positions. It dismissed an application for annulment of a Commission decision prohibiting a concentration involving Gencor Ltd, a South African mining company and Lonrho plc. The basis of the CFI's decision was that the concentration would have led to the creation of a dominant oligopoly position between the entity resulting from the concentration and another company in the world platinum and rhodium markets, as a result of which effective competition would have been significantly impeded in the common market. The ECJ also ruled on collective dominance in *France v Commission/SCPE* and *EMC v Commission* (Joined Cases C-68/94 & C-30/95). However, in this case the ECJ held that the Commission had misapplied the concept by failing to establish that the concentration in question would in fact give rise to a collective dominant position in the relevant market. The Commission decision was annulled.

Key Principle: **A full economic analysis is necessary before the Commission can reach a decision in relation to a proposed merger.**

Airtours Plc v Commission (Case T-342/99) 2002
Airtours (A), a UK company selling package holidays to short haul destinations such as Spain and Italy, launched a bid to take

over First Choice (FC). FC was one of A's main UK competitors, the others being Thomsons (T) and Thomas Cook (TC). The bid was notified to the Commission which found in September 1999 that it was incompatible with the common market as it would give the merged company, along with T and TC collective dominance; leading to higher prices, restricted market capacity and increased profits. The Commission considered that the bid would increase the share of A, T and TC in the short haul market from 68 per cent to 78 per cent. A challenged the decision of the Commission before the CFI.

Held: (CFI): The Commission had failed to prove that the merger would have adverse effects on competition, owing to a series of errors as to whether a collective dominant position might be created.

Commentary

(1) The errors arose (to a substantial degree) as a result of the Commission's approach to economic analysis before it reached a decision. The Commission considered (wrongly) that customers did not switch between short and long haul holidays, thus reaching a wrong decision about the market.

(2) The CFI identified three conditions that must be met before a finding of collective dominance may be made:

(a) Given the characteristics of the relevant market, each member of the oligopoly must know how the other members are behaving in order to be able to adopt the same policy.

(b) Members of the oligopoly must be deterred over time from departing from the policy thus adopted.

(c) That policy must be able to withstand challenge by other competitors, potential competitors or customers.

Overturning the Commission decision, the CFI found that the Commission had not established that the three leading tour operators would have an incentive to stop competing with each other. Contrary to the view of the Commission, consumers may exercise significant buying power, switching to other operators or destinations in response to price rises.

(3) The CFI overturned two further Commission decisions onproposed mergers in *Schneider Electric SA v Commission* (Case T-310/01) and *Tetra Laval BV v Commission* (Cases

T-5/02 and T-80/02), both in October 2002. The Commission was found to have failed to produce sufficient evidence in its economic analysis of the anti-competitive effects of both proposed mergers. The ECJ upheld the decision of the CFI on appeal in *Commission v Tetra Laval* (Case C-12/03P and C-13/03P).

(4) The Commission was concerned at the implications of three major decision being overturned in the CFI in this way. In December it adopted a comprehensive package in relation to EU merger control. The central element of the package is a new merger regulation, which amended and recast Regulation 4064/89. Key features of the new Regulation seek to:

   (a) Clarify that the Merger regulation may apply to situations of oligopoly which may give rise to competition problems.
   (b) Rationalise the timing of applications to the Commission for proposed mergers.
   (c) Simplify the system for transfer of cases between Commission and national competition authorities.
   (d) Introduce greater flexibility especially into the investigation of complex cases.
   (e) Strengthen the investigative powers of the Commission.

(5) Other elements of the merger reform package include the appointment of a Chief Competition Economist within the Commission to provide advice on mergers and other competition investigations, the adoption of a notice on mergers between competing firms and speedy review by the courts of merger decisions.

Enforcement of the competition rules

Key Principle: **Investigations into breaches of competition law may be either compulsory or voluntary.**

National Panasonic (UK) Ltd v Commission (Case 136/79) 1980
Suspecting an infringement (a concerted practice) of Art.81 (ex 85), the Commission carried out a compulsory investigation of National Panasonic (UK) without warning.

Held: (ECJ) The Commission was entitled under Art.14 of Reg.17 to investigate without prior notice where a breach was suspected. A concerted practice was found. [1980] E.C.R. 2033.

Commentary

(1) This investigation was carried out under Regulation 17/62, now replaced by Regulation 1/2003.

(2) Under Regulation 1/2003, Art.20, the Commission continues to be empowered to inspect premises. The main change under the new Regulation is the requirement for the Commission to consult NCAs before making a decision to investigate.

(3) Powers of entry and search relate only to the undertaking and not to the individual. Thus, they enable the Commission to enter the business premises of an undertaking under suspicion, but not to enter the home of, say, one of the directors, even if they believe that the individual has removed papers to his home. See *Hoechst v Commission* (Joined Cases 46 & 227/88) in which the search of the home premises of a senior member of staff was found to be illegal, being in breach of the principle of the inviolability of the home, contrary to the European Convention of Human Rights. See also *Orkem v Commission* (Case 374/87) and *Dow Benelux N.V. v Commission* (Case 85/87), the latter upholding the decision in *Hoechst*.

(4) Investigations may also be voluntary under Art.13.

Key Principle: **The ECJ must have regard to the legitimate business interests of undertakings in protection of their business secrets and must not disclose information acquired to the national authorities.**

Adams v Commission (Case 145/83) 1985

The Commission disclosed information about Adams, an informant, to the Swiss authorities, as a result of which A was charged and convicted by the Swiss courts. (For full facts, see Ch.6, p.72).

Held: (ECJ) The Commission was liable for breach of the principle of confidentiality (although damages were reduced by A's contributory negligence).

Commentary

See also *Australian Mining & Smelting Co Ltd v Commission* (Case 155/79): limited professional privilege applies to communications between lawyer and client.

Key Principle: **As Arts 81 and 82 are directly effective, they may be enforced in the national courts.**

Cutsforth v Mansfield Inns 1986

C sought to rely on Art.81 (ex 85) in relation to a term in agreement between the tenants of tied houses and the brewer which had taken over the chain of public houses. Under the agreement the tenants would only be permitted to obtain their equipment from authorised suppliers. C, who had previously supplied gaming equipment to the public houses, was not authorised.

Held: (HC) There was a serious prima facie case between the parties. An interlocutory order restraining the application of the offending term was granted. [1986] 1 C.M.L.R. 1.

Commentary

(1) Although it was suggested in *Garden Cottage Foods v Milk Marketing Board* (HL 1983) that damages should be available for breach of Art.86 (now 82) the position was not made clear in that case. Subsequently, the *Francovich* decision (Joined Cases C-6/90 & 9/90) has established that Member States are liable in damages for breaches of EC law (see Ch.1, p.13).

(2) The implementation of Regulation 1/2003 has completely changed the power of the national courts to apply EC competition law. Under Art.6 of the Regulation, national courts will be able to apply Art.81 in its entirety, including Art.81(3). They must, however, under Art.10, seek to avoid making a decision which conflicts with a Commission decision: Art.16. In the event of uncertainty, national courts

may (as they could under existing law) make a preliminary reference under Art.234. They may also ask the Commission to provide information in its possession: Art.15(1), or for an opinion on the application of EC competition rules. The Commission may submit observations before the national courts on Arts 81 and 82 on matters of EC interest.

14. EQUAL PAY AND TREATMENT

Equal pay

Key Principle: **Member States must ensure and maintain the application of the principle that men and women receive equal pay for equal work: Art.141 (ex 119).**

Defrenne v Sabena (Case 43/75) 1976
For facts, see Ch.1, p.8.

Held: **(ECJ) Art.119 (now 141) is directly effective from the date of the judgment (April 8, 1976). [1976] E.C.R. 455.**

Commentary

(1) Equal pay claims within Art.141 may be enforced againstboth public and private bodies, as Treaty provisions are effective both vertically and horizontally. By contrast, equal treatment claims under the relevant directive may only be enforced against public bodies as directives are vertically but not horizontally effective (see p.8).

(2) The original economic emphasis of the Treaty of Rome hasshifted towards a greater recognition of the social dimension. In *Deutsche Post Ag v Sievers and Schrage* (Joined Cases C-270 & 271/97) the ECJ held that the economic aim pursued by Art.141 is secondary to the social aim under the Article, which constitutes the expression of a fundamental human right.

Key Principle: **"Pay" means the ordinary basic or minimum wage or salary and any other consideration, in cash or kind, which the worker receives, directly or indirectly, in respect of his employment: Art.141.**

Worringham v Lloyds Bank Ltd (Case 69/80)
Lloyds Bank operated two retirement schemes, one for men and one for women. Male employees under 25, but not female

employees, received a notional additional sum for the purpose of calculating the level of employer contributions towards pension entitlement.

Held: (ECJ) Even though the payment was notional and was immediately removed to the pension scheme, it was "pay" under Art.141 (ex 119). [1981] E.C.R. 767.

Commentary

(1) The payment in Worringham was "pay" because it was repaid to employees leaving the scheme early and was included in gross pay to calculate other entitlements such as redundancy pay.

(2) The grant of special travel facilities to former employees was held to be "pay" in *Garland v BREL* (Case 12/81).

(3) Contributions paid into a statutory social security scheme are not pay: *Defrenne v Belgian State* (Case 80/70), upheld in *Barber v GRE.* (Case 262/88), unlike contributions paid into an occupational pension scheme, which are covered by Art.141 (see p.175).

(4) A judicial award of compensation for breach for the right not to be unfairly dismissed is pay under Art.141: *R. v Secretary of State for Employment, Ex p. Seymour-Smith and Perez* (Case C-167/97) (see p.178).

Maternity schemes

Key Principle: **To assess the maternity scheme of a public body it is necessary to consider the scheme in relation to Art.141, Directive 75/117 on equal pay and equal treatment, Directive 76/207 on equal treatment and Directive 92/85 which is intended to improve the safety and health at work of pregnant workers and workers who have recently given birth or are breastfeeding.**

Boyle v Equal Opportunities Commission (Case C-411/96)
B and six others were employed by the EOC and were of childbearing age. They had all worked at the EOC for more than one year and were not employed on casual or short-notice or fixed term (of less than two years) contracts. At least three had

recently taken maternity leave. They sought a declaration before an industrial tribunal that the maternity scheme operated by their employers contravened Art.141 (ex 119) and the three Directives (75/117, 76/207 and 92/85). The tribunal referred questions to the ECJ under Art.234 (ex 177).

Held: (ECJ) (1) A clause in a contract of employment making the application maternity scheme which is more favourable than the statutory scheme conditional on the pregnant woman's return to work after the birth of the child or repay the difference between statutory and occupational scheme was not discriminatory.

(2) Although the right to the minimum period of 14 weeks' maternity leave provided for by the Directive may be waived by the worker (apart from the two weeks' compulsory maternity leave), if a woman becomes ill during statutory maternity leave and moves to more favourable sick leave which terminates before the maternity leave, the period of maternity leave remains unaffected by the sick leave. [1998] ECR I-6401.

Commentary
A lump sum payment made exclusively to female workers who take maternity leave where the payment is designed to offset the occupational disadvantages arising for workers due to their absence from work is pay under Art.141. However, as male and female workers are in different situations, there is no breach of Art.141: *Abdoulaye v Regie Nationale des Usines Renault SA* (Case C-219/98). Note that maternity pay should not be so low as to undermine the protective purpose of leave: *Gillespie v Northern Ireland Health and Social Services Board* (Case C-342/93). Any pay rise awarded to a woman on maternity leave between the beginning of the and the end of the maternity leave in the period covered by the reference pay should be treated as pay under Art.141 and must be included in the elements of pay taken into account in calculating the amount of maternity pay: *Alabaster v Woolwich Plc, Ex p. Secretary of State for Social Security* (Case C-147/02).

Part-time workers

Key Principle: **Exclusion of part-time workers from entitlements such as sick pay may contravene Art.141 where there are more female than male part-timers.**

Rinner-Kuhn v FWW (Case 171/88) 1989
Part-time employees whose contracts limited their work to 10 hours a week or 45 hours a month were excluded from entitlement to sick pay.

Held: (ECJ) As more women than men worked part time, such a restriction infringed Art.141 (ex 119) unless it was objectively justified. [1989] E.C.R. 2743.

Commentary
The ECJ rejected as inadequate the "justification" of the German Government that part-time workers were less integrated into their employment and upheld its decision in *Bilka Kaufhaus* (Case 170/84) (see pp.177 & 181).

Key Principle: **Art.141 and Directive 75/117 apply to part-time workers in the United Kingdom, enabling them to claim for redundancy pay on the same terms as full-timers under United Kingdom law.**

R. v Secretary of State for Employment, Ex p. EOC 1994
The Equal Opportunities Commission (EOC) brought an action in the United Kingdom courts claiming that provisions for redundancy under United Kingdom law infringed Art.141 (ex 119) and Directive 75/117 and that the conditions governing conditions for unfair dismissal for part-time workers infringed Directive 76/207 on equal treatment (see p.190).

Held: (HL) The exclusion of part-time workers from redundancy benefits and protection against unfair dismissal infringed Art.141 (ex 119), Directive 75/117 and Directive 76/207 respectively. [1995] A.C. 1.

Commentary
The United Kingdom has given effect to this decision in the Employment Rights Act 1996.

Occupational pensions

Key Principle: **Payments under occupational pensions schemes are "pay" under Art.141.**

Barber v Guardian Royal Exchange (Case C-262/88) 1990

Mr Barber belonged to a pension fund established by his employers, Guardian Royal Exchange. The scheme was non-contributory and "contracted out" (i.e. a private, non-statutory scheme approved by UK law). Under the scheme women were entitled to receive their pension at the age of 57 years, whereas men had to wait until they were 62. In the event of redundancy women received an immediate payment at 50 and men at 55. Mr Barber was made redundant at the age of 52. He received severance pay, statutory redundancy pay and an ex gratia payment, but was told that he would not receive his pension until he reached pensionable age (i.e. 62 years). Mr Barber brought proceedings in an industrial tribunal based on the Sex Discrimination Act, claiming unlawful discrimination. (A woman in his position would have received an immediate pension.) His action initially failed but reached the Court of Appeal in appeal proceedings brought by his widow after Mr Barber's death. The Court of Appeal referred questions to the ECJ.

Held: (ECJ) (1) A pension paid under a contracted out, private occupational scheme is "pay" under Art.141 (ex 119).

(2) It is a breach of Art.141 (ex 119) in a contracted-out scheme to impose an age condition which differs between men and women, even where permissible under national law. To enable national courts to identify and eliminate any discrimination between the sexes, all elements of a remuneration package must be transparent.

(3) Equality in pension claims may only be claimed from the date of the judgment (May 17, 1990) except for claims initiated before the judgment. [1990] E.C.R. I-1889.

Commentary

(1) Barber has been an immensely important decision as it has required occupational pension schemes to harmonise the retirement ages for men and women. Before equality measures are taken, equalisation must be achieved without

reducing existing entitlements. After measures are taken, equality may be fixed at any level: *Van den Akker v Stichting Shell Pensioenfonds* (Case C-28/93).

(2) The ECJ limited the temporal effect of the judgment, as it did in *Defrenne*. This restriction was confirmed in a protocol to the Maastricht Treaty.

(3) The *Barber* decision has caused Directive 86/378 (Equal Treatment in Occupational Pensions Schemes) to lose significance, as most issues relating to differences between men and women in retirement ages or pension entitlement are now covered by Art.141.

(4) Pensions paid to the spouses of deceased employees are within Art.141: *Ten Oever v Stichting Bedriffspensioenfonds Voor Het Glazenwassers* (Case C-109/91).

(5) The arrangements for funding occupational pensions areoutside Art.141, thus permitting schemes to require different levels of contribution from men and women based on actuarial factors such as life expectancy: *Neath v Hugh Steeper* (Case C-152/91). Statutory social security schemes are also outside Art.141: *Barber*; as are "single sex" schemes: *Coloroll Pension Trustees Ltd v Russell* (Case C-200/91).

(6) The ECJ in *Deutsche Telekom v Schröder* (Case C-50/96) and other joined cases found that exclusion of part-time workers from an occupational pension scheme amounted to discrimination contrary to (old) Art.119, if the measure affects a considerably higher percentage of female than male workers, unless objectively justified. (This is known as indirect discrimination. See *Seymour Smith*, below.)

(7) Another instance of indirect discrimination in relation to pensions arose in *Preston v Fletcher* (Case C-78/98). This time the workers in question were prevented from pursuing their claim for retrospective membership of the pension scheme by a national (UK) law requiring them to bring their claim within six months of completing their employment and restricted the period of retrospective membership of the pension scheme to the two years before their claim was instituted. The Court found that the six month requirement for a claim did not infringe EC law, since it supported the principle of effectiveness and legal certainty. The restriction of membership, however, did contravene the principle of

effectiveness since it excluded from the record of service the period before the two year point.

(8) In *Griesmar* (Case C-366/99) the ECJ found that exclusion of civil servants who are fathers from entitlement to the service credits paid to retired civil servants who are mothers infringes the principle of equal pay if the fathers can prove that they brought up the children.

(9) In *Menaur* (Case C-379/99) the ECJ interpreted old Art.119 as meaning that bodies such as German pension funds entrusted with providing an occupational pension scheme must ensure equal treatment for men and women, even if the employees discriminated against have a protected right against their employers in the event of insolvency that excludes all discrimination.

Direct and indirect discrimination

Key Principle: **Direct discrimination is illegal under Art.141. Indirect discrimination may be legal if it is objectively justified.**

Bilka-Kaufhaus GmbH v Weber von Hartz (Case 170/84) 1980
Part-time workers were excluded from an occupational pension scheme unless they had been employed for 15 years. Full time employees were not similarly restricted. As nearly all the parttimers were female, the effects were felt disproportionally by women. A female part-timer challenged the exclusion in the German courts, which made a reference to the ECJ.

Held: (ECJ) (1) Exclusion of part-time workers from a pension scheme infringes Art.141 (ex 119) where: (a) a considerably smaller proportion of the workforce is employed part-time; (b) the difference in treatment is based on sex; and (c) the exclusion is not objectively justified.

(2) A measure will be objectively justified if it corresponds to a real need on the part of the undertaking, it is appropriate to achieve the objective pursued and it is necessary. [1986] E.C.R. 110.

Commentary

(1) Direct discrimination occurs where one sex is treated disadvantageously compared with the other sex. (See *Dekker v Stichtung Vormingscentrum Voor Jonge Volwassenen* (Case

C-177/88), discrimination on grounds of pregnancy was held to be direct discrimination.)

(2) Indirect discrimination involves practices which are not apparently discriminatory but which have an adverse effect which is felt disproportionately by one sex, as in the exclusion of the part-time (female) employees from the pension scheme in *Bilka-Kaufhaus*, upholding the earlier decision in *Jenkins v Kingsgate* (Clothing Productions) Ltd (Case 96/80) (paying part-time employees, most of whom were female, less than men did not infringe Art.141 (ex 119) if objectively justified and not based on discrimination on grounds of sex).

(3) In the United Kingdom the House of Lords ruled in *R. v Secretary of State for Employment, Ex p. EOC* (HL, 1994) that the requirement for part-time workers to be employed for five years (compared with two years for full-time workers) before gaining certain employment protection rights was indirect discrimination which was not objectively justified.

Key Principle: **In assessing whether a measure adopted by a Member State has a disparate effect on men and women so as to amount to indirect discrimination, the state should consider the respective proportions of men in the workforce able to satisfy the requirement and those unable to do so, and compare these proportions as regards women in the workforce.**

R. v Secretary of State for Employment, Ex p. Seymour Smithand Perez (Case C-167/97)
The applicants were two women, each of whom had been dismissed from their employment before completing the two year period required for protection against unfair dismissal under a UK Order of 1985. They claimed before the Divisional Court that the Order was indirectly discriminatory against women, contrary to the Equal Treatment Directive 76/207, and before the Court of Appeal, that the Order infringed Art.141 (ex 119). After a misleading declaration by the CA, the House of Lords requested a ruling from the ECJ under Art.234 (ex 177).

Held: (ECJ) It is for the national courts to assess the factors and reach a conclusion. The onus was on the Member State to show that:

(1) The alleged discriminatory rule reflected a legitimate aim of social policy.

(2) The aim was unrelated to any discrimination based on sex.

(3) The Member State could reasonably consider that the means chosen were suitable for attaining that aim.

Commentary

(1) The House of Lords applied the ruling in February 2000. After analysing the statistics it held that the impact of the UK legislation was debatable but that, at the time of the action, it was objectively justified. The HL decision was, by then, overtaken by events, as the two-year qualification period had been abolished.

(2) A national rule limiting entitlement under Art.141 (ex 119) to two years before the commencement of proceedings had the effect of preventing proper enjoyment of EC law rights: *Magorrian v Eastern Health and Social Services Board* (Case C-246/96).

(3) While it is for the national courts to lay down detailed rules on the protection of employment rights under EC law, such rules may not be less favourable than those covering comparable domestic claims and may not make it virtually impossible to exercise those rights: *Levez v T.H. Jennings (Harlow Pools) Ltd* (Case C-326/96). The ECJ held that, where an employer misinformed a female employee as to the salary of her male predecessor, a restriction on arrears of pay to two years prior to the commencement of proceedings could not be applied.

Key Principle: **Men and women have equal rights to join an occupational pension scheme under Art.141.**

Dietz v Stichting Thuiszorg Rotterdam (Case C-435/93) 1996
Dietz was employed by the defendants part-time until November 6, 1990 when she agreed to retire early at the age of 61. At that time part-timers were excluded from occupational pension schemes. She claimed she would have retired later if she had

known about imminent changes to the pension scheme of benefit to her. The Dutch court made a reference to the ECJ.

Held: (ECJ) The right to join an occupational pension scheme is covered by Art.141 (ex 119) and can be enforced against the scheme's administrators. [1997] 1 C.M.L.R. 199.

Commentary

(1) The ECJ in *Dietz* followed *Vroege v NCIV Institut Voor Volkshuisvesting* (Case C-57/93) in placing no restrictions on the temporal effect of Art.141 (ex 119) in this context (cf. Barber). However it ruled that national time limits may be invoked in relation to Art.141 (ex 119) provided the limits are no less favourable than those relating to comparable domestic actions.

(2) On equality of access to pension schemes, see also *Fisscher v Voorhuis Hengelo* (Case C-128/93) where the exclusion of married women from an occupational scheme was found to infringe Art.141 (ex 119).

Redundancy pay

Barber v GRE (Case C-262/88)

For facts, see p.175, above.

Held: (ECJ) Redundancy pay is "pay" under Art.141 (ex 119), whether paid under a contract of employment, by virtue of legislative provisions or on a voluntary basis.

Commentary

After *Barber*, the earlier decision of the ECJ in *Burton v British Railways Board* (Case 19/81) would appear to have little relevance. In *Burton* the ECJ held that discrimination between the sexes in terms of age of entitlement to voluntary redundancy was calculated by reference to the statutory retirement age (60 for women and 65 for men). As Directive 79/7 (see p.177) permitted Member States to exclude the statutory retirement age from equal treatment, the claim under Directive 76/207 failed. Such a claim could now be brought under Art.141. United Kingdom law permitting different statutory retirement ages for men and women was amended by the Sex Discrimination Act 1986 which made discrimination between the sexes in retirement ages illegal and by the Employment Act 1989 which provides for a single retirement age of 65 years for both sexes for redundancy benefit.

Equal work

Key Principle: **Equal pay for equal work means the elimination of all discrimination on grounds of sex for the same work or for work to which an equal value is attributed, with regard to all aspects and conditions of remuneration: Art.1, Directive 75/117.**

Bilka-Kaufhaus GmbH v Webervon Hertz (Case C-170/84) 1986
For facts and decision, see p.177, above.

Commentary

(1) Directive 75/117 was adopted to clarify Art.141 (ex 141) and to provide a mechanism for comparing work of equal value. It does not alter the scope of Art.141 (ex 119): *Jenkins v Kingsgate* (Case 96/80) (see above). Thus, all considerations applying to Art.141 also apply to Directive 75/117, including the decisions of the ECJ on direct and indirect discrimination and on objective justification (see pp.177–180).

(2) Where men and women are engaged in the same work, as in *Bilka-Kaufhaus* and *Jenkins v Kingsgate* (see p.177), discrimination infringes Art.141 where it is based exclusively on the difference of sex of the worker.

(3) Where statistics show a significant difference in pay for jobs of equal value where one (in this case pharmacy) is carried out almost exclusively by men and the other (speech therapy) by women, the employer must establish that the difference is objectively justified by factors other than sex: *Enderby v Frenchay Area Health Authority and Secretary of State for Health* (Case C-127/92).

(4) Where people perform seemingly identical tasks but draw on knowledge and different skills and who do not have the same qualifications to perform other tasks that may be assigned to them, they do not do the "same work" for the

purpose of Art.141 (ex 119): *Angestelltenbetriebsrat der Wiener Gebietskrankencasse* (Case C-309/97). In this case social insurance institutions in Austria employed three different classes of psychotherapists, paid at different rates: doctors, graduate psychologists and others with a specialised training in psychology.

(5) See also *Brunnhofer v Bank der Österreichen* (Case C-381/99) in which it was held that it is not permissible to put together the personal qualities of the employee with the way in which she worked in order to support the view that she was not engaged in similar work or work of equal value to the work of other employees.

Key Principle: **Equal work need not be identical work but must display a high degree of similarity.**

Macarthys Ltd v Smith (Case 129/79) 1981
Mrs Smith was appointed by Macarthys as a warehouse manager. She complained that she was paid less than her male predecessor, who had left four months before she took up the job. The Court of Appeal made a reference to the ECJ to clarify the meaning of Art.141 (ex 119) in such circumstances.

Held: (ECJ) The principle of equal pay for equal work is not confined to situations where men and women are contemporaneously doing equal work for the same employer.

Commentary
While the ECJ did not rule in *Macarthys* on the meaning of "the same work", Advocate General Caportorti submitted that it included jobs which were highly similar but not identical. There must always be a real (not hypothetical) comparator, even if that comparator is not employed at the same time.

Work of equal value

Key Principle: **Where a job classification scheme is used to determine pay, it must be based on the same criteria for men and women, and must exclude discrimination based on sex: Art.1(2), Directive 75/117.**

Rummler v Dato Druck (Case 237/85) 1986
The applicant challenged the criteria under a job classification scheme, claiming that she should have been placed in a higher paid category covering heavy physical work, because packing parcels was a heavy task for her. The employer considered that the job placed only light physical demands on her. A reference was made to the ECJ.

Held: (ECJ) (1) A job classification scheme based on strength or physical hardship does not infringe Directive 75/117 provided the system precludes discrimination on grounds of sex and that the criteria employed are objectively justified. (2) "Objectively justified" means appropriate to the tasks to be carried out and corresponding to a genuine need of the undertaking.

Commentary

(1) The ECJ in *Rummler* approached the issue as one of indirect discrimination, which may be capable of objective justification. It would be discriminatory to calculate the physical effort required for a job by reference to the average characteristics of one sex. However, the applicant's subjective experience of effort was not relevant.

(2) The criteria in a job evaluation scheme must be "transparent" (i.e. clearly displayed): *Handels-Og Kontorfunktionaernesforbund v Dansk Arbejdsgivforening for Danfoss* (Case 109/88). (If the criterion of "flexibility" meant quality of work, it was neutral unless it systematically discriminated against women. If it meant adaptability to work schedules it could discriminate against women due to their family responsibilities.) Each element in a remuneration package will need separate consideration in an equal value claim. See also *Barber*: pp.175 & 180.

(3) In *Lawrence v Regent Office Care Ltd* (Case C-320/00) the applicants were Mr Lawrence and 446 other workers employed as cleaners, nearly all women. Female workers had brought an action against Regent Office which led to a ruling in the HL, stating that their work was of equal value to the male workers. As a result, pay for women increased. The appellants were workers employed by the respondent undertakings, and who were regarded as performing work of equal value. The Court held that, as a result, the work

and payment of these workers could not be compared. Where the differences identified in the pay conditions of workers of different sex performing equal work or work of equal value cannot be attributed to a single source, the situation is not covered by Art.141.

Key Principle: **Member States must provide a means of assessing equal value claims if they do not provide a job classification scheme.**

Commission v UK (Re Equal Pay for Equal Work) (Case 61/81) 1982
United Kingdom law provided for equal pay for people doing "like work" or work rated as equivalent in a job evaluation scheme. Such schemes were only instituted with the agreement of the employer. The Commission brought proceedings against the United Kingdom in the ECJ under Art.226 (ex 169).

Held: (ECJ) (1) Job classification is only one of several ways to determine equal value.

(2) United Kingdom's interpretation of Directive 75/117denies the existence of the right to equal pay for work of equal value where no classification has been made, contrary to the general scheme and provisions of the Directive. [1982] E.C.R. 2601.

Commentary
Under Art.6 of the directive, Member States must take the necessary measures to ensure that the principle of equal pay is applied. Effective means must be available (not necessarily by a job classification scheme).

Equal treatment

Key Principle: **Men and women are entitled to be treated equally as regards access to employment, including promotion, and to vocational training and as regards working conditions and social security: Art.1, Equal Treatment Directive 76/207 (amended by Directive 2002/73).**

Key Principle: **There shall be no discrimination on grounds of sex in the conditions, including selection criteria, for access to all jobs or posts, whatever the sector or branch of activity, and to all levels of the occupational hierarchy: Art.3, Directive 76/207.**

Dekker v Stichtung Vormingscentrum Voor Jonge Volwassen Plus (Case 177/88) 1990

Ms D applied for a job at a youth training centre in the Netherlands. Although the selection committee considered Ms D to be the most suitable applicant for the post she was not offered employment because she was pregnant. (The centre's insurers had refused to reimburse sickness benefits in the event of taking on an employee known to be pregnant.) The Dutch courts referred questions to the ECJ under Art.234 (ex 177).

Held: (ECJ) Discrimination based on pregnancy was direct discrimination contrary to Art.3 of Directive 76/207. [1990] E.C.R. I-3941.

Commentary

(1) The wording of Art.3 was amended and extended by Directive 2002/73 (from October 2005).

(2) There was no need in *Dekker* to compare the position of men and women, since women alone may be refused employment because they are pregnant. Such a refusal is therefore direct discrimination and incapable of objective justification.

(3) By contrast, where a woman becomes ill as a complication of pregnancy and is dismissed, the ECJ has held that the dismissal is indirect discrimination and is thus capable of objective justification: *Handels-Og Kontorfunktionaerer-Nes Forbund I Denmark (Acting for Hertz) v Dansk Arbejdsgiv-forening* (Case 179/88).

(4) In *Mahlburg* (Case C-207/98) the ECJ ruled that Directive 76/207 precludes a refusal to appoint a pregnant woman to a post for an indefinite period on the ground that a statutory prohibition on employment attaching to pregnancy prevents her from being employed in that post from the outset and for the duration of pregnancy.

Pregnancy and maternity

Key Principle: **There shall be no discrimination on grounds of sex either directly or indirectly by reference in particular to marital or family status: Art.2(1) of Directive 76/207.**

Key Principle: **The directive shall be without prejudice to provisions concerning the protection of women, particularly as regards pregnancy and maternity: Art.2(7).**

Webb v EMO Air Cargo (UK) Ltd (Case C-32/93) 1994

This decision concerned a woman who was dismissed when she became pregnant while employed on an indefinite term during the maternity leave of another employee: see Ch.1, p.12. The fundamental issue was whether she was unlawfully dismissed. Ms Webb claimed that the dismissal amounted to discrimination contrary to s.1 of the Sex Discrimination Act 1975 and that the Act should be interpreted subject to the Equal Treatment Directive 76/207. The House of Lords decided to refer questions for interpretation of the directive to the ECJ under Art.234 (ex 177). [1994] E.C.R. I-3567.

Held: (ECJ) Art.2(1) read with Art.5(1) of Directive 76/207 precludes dismissal of an employee who is recruited for an unlimited term with a view, initially, to replacing another employee during the latter's maternity leave and who cannot do so because, shortly after recruitment, she herself is found to be pregnant. [1994] E.C.R. I-3567.

Commentary

(1) The ECJ ruled that no comparison should be made between the situation of a woman incapable of working due to pregnancy and a man similarly incapable for medical or other reasons. Pregnancy is not a pathological condition comparable to non-availability for work on non-medical grounds (which would otherwise justify dismissal without discrimination on grounds of sex).

(2) The ruling makes it clear that dismissal of a pregnant woman recruited for an indefinite period cannot be justified on grounds related to her inability to fulfil a fundamental

condition of her employment contract. The wording appeared to provide a loophole allowing dismissal in circumstances where a woman becomes pregnant having been engaged for a definite period of time (e.g. as a maternity leave replacement).

(3) This anomaly was resolved by the Directive 92/85 on pregnant workers and working mothers, which provides protection for all pregnant employees against dismissal, regardless of the nature of contractual service. The directive does not cover refusal to employ a pregnant woman. However, in *Mahlburg v Land Meckleburg-Vorpommern* (Case C-207/98) refusal to appoint a pregnant woman for an indefinite period in line with a national prohibition, was found to be in breach of Directive 92/85. Art.5 of Directive 76/207 was deleted by Directive 2002/73.

(4) See also *Melgar v Ayuntamiento de Los Barrios* (Case C-438/99) and *Tele Danmark A/S* (Case C-109/00). M had been recruited by the municipality of Los Barrios in Spain for three months, her contract being renewed twice. After signing a fourth contract for a fixed-term on a part-time basis in May 1999, she was issued with a letter stating that her contract would terminate in June 1999. She was pregnant at the time and gave birth in September 1999. M brought proceedings in the national courts against the municipality, leading to referral under Art.234. *Tele Danmark A/S* (Case C-109/00) also involved an employee on a fixed-term contract (six months, in this case) who was dismissed on account of pregnancy. Tele Danmark claimed that the applicant should have informed them that she was due to give birth before the end of the six month period. Clarification was sought by the Danish court under Art.234. The ECJ held (in *Melgar*) that the prohibition on the dismissal of pregnant women applies to both fixed-term and part-time appointments. In *Tele Danmark* the ECJ confirmed that a refusal of employment on account of pregnancy cannot be justified by financial loss which the employer may suffer, if he recruits a woman during her maternity leave or because the woman he has recruited cannot occupy the post during her pregnancy.

(5) In the UK the Employment Rights Act 1996, s.99 provides that it is automatically unfair to dismiss a woman, irrespective of her hours of work or length of service, if the reason

for dismissal is that she is pregnant or for any other reason connected with her pregnancy.

(6) The House of Lords' ruling on the duty to interpret national law to accord with Directive 76/207 and its subsequent decision applying the Art.234 (ex 177) ruling are considered in Ch.1, p.12: *Webb v EMO*.

(7) Applying the principle of non-discrimination, pregnant workers require protection against unfair dismissal throughout the period of pregnancy: *Brown v Rentokil* (Case 394/96).

Key Principle: **Men and women must be guaranteed the same working conditions, including conditions governing dismissal: Art.5 of Directive 76/207.**

Marshall v Southampton and South West Hampshire Area Health Authority (No.1) (Case 152/84) 1986
For facts, see Ch.1, p.9.

Held: (ECJ) Art.5 of Directive 76/207 does not entitle Member States to limit the application of the equal treatment principle and may be relied upon by an individual against the state before the national courts. [1986] E.C.R. 723.

Commentary

(1) Ms Marshall could rely on Art.5 of the Directive against a public body, the Area Health Authority when compelled to retire at an earlier age than her male counterparts (a practice permitted at that time in the United Kingdom under the Sex Discrimination Act 1975). The *Marshall* decision is important most notably because the ECJ confirmed that directives may have vertical but not horizontal effect. Art.5 was deleted by Directive 2002/73.

(2) The retirement age for receiving an occupational pension is not necessarily the same as the age of entitlement to state retirement benefits. The exception in the Social Security Directive 79/7 (permitting different ages for the receipt of state pensions for men and women) must be interpreted

strictly so as to be inapplicable to the fixing of retirement ages under occupational pension schemes.

(3) This approach was confirmed in *Roberts v Tate and Lyle Ltd* (Case 151/84) in relation to the fixing of different retirement ages for both sexes under an early retirement scheme, held to be illegal under Art.5 of Directive 76/207.

Remedies

Key Principle: **Member States must introduce into their legal systems the necessary procedures and remedies to enforce the equal treatment principle: Art.6 of Directive 76/207.**

Von Colson and Kamann v Land Nordheim Westfalen (Case 14/83) 1984
For facts, see Ch.1, p.10.

Held: (ECJ) While Art.6 of the directive does not satisfy the requirements for direct effect, Member States are obliged by the principle of effectiveness to interpret national law to comply with the relevant EC Directive. [1984] E.C.R. 1891.

Commentary

(1) In the context of Art.6 of the directive, the obligation under *Von Colson* is for national authorities to interpret implementing legislation so as to ensure that it provides for appropriate procedures and remedies.

(2) See *Marshall v Southampton and South West Area Health Authority (No.2)* (Case C-271/91) in which the ECJ held that Art.6 was directly effective and was infringed where a Member State imposed an upper limit on compensation in relation to EC law. The effect of this ruling was to remove the ceiling previously applied by industrial tribunals in equal treatment claims.

(3) Note that Art.6 has been amended by Directive 2002/73.

Exceptions to the equal treatment principle

Key Principle: **Member States may exclude from the operation of the equal treatment principle, occupational activities
and training where the sex of the worker is a determining
factor, provided the objective is legitimate and the means,
proportionate: Art.2(6) of Directive 2002/73.**

Commission v UK (Re Equal Treatment of Men and Women) (Case 165/82) 1983

The Commission brought enforcement proceedings against the
United Kingdom under Art.226 (ex 169) in relation to the
implementation of Directive 76/207. The claim contained three
main complaints:

(1) United Kingdom legislation failed to provide that collec-
    tive and other agreements which contravened the
    principle of equal treatment were void;

(2) the exclusion under s.6(3) of the Sex Discrimination 1975
    Act from the equal treatment of employment in private
    households or where five or fewer individuals were
    employed infringed Directive 76/207;

(3) s.20 of the 1975 Act wrongly excluded midwives from the
    equal treatment principle.

Held: (ECJ) The United Kingdom was found to be in breach of
EC law in relation to the first two complaints, but not the third,
due to the sensitivity of the midwife/patient relationship. [1983]
E.C.R. 3431.

Commentary

Art.2(7) (previously Art.2(3)) allows an exception for the protection of women, particularly during pregnancy and maternity. This
right has been extended to cover women who adopt children, but
not men: *Commission v Italy* (Case 163/82). A similar distinction
between the sexes was taken in *Hofmann v Barmer Ersatzkasse*
(Case 184/83) in which extra maternity leave granted to mothers
was not extended to fathers, the leave recognising both the
biological condition of giving birth and the relationship between
mother and child.

Equal treatment and the armed forces.

Key Principle: **National decisions on the management of the armed forces must normally observe the principle of equal treatment between men and women.**

Johnston and the Chief Constable of the RUC (Case 222/84)
J, a female member of the RUC, challenged the RUC's refusal to renew her contract, as it had made a policy decision not to train women in the use of firearms.

Held: (ECJ) Any claim to depart from Directive 76/207 must be decided by the national court only in the light of the Directive and not in the light of Art.39(3). [1986] E.C.R. 1651.

Commentary

(1) In *Sirdar v the Army Board and Secretary of State for Defence* (Case C-273/97) the applicant was a woman excluded from joining the Royal Marines. Unlike other units of the British armed forces, each individual, regardless of specialisation, must be able to serve at any time in a commando unit. The ECJ held that the Royal Marines were combat units pursuing activities for which sex is a determining factor.

(2) In *Kreil v Bundesrepublik Deutschland* (Case C-285/98) the ECJ considered a national (German) exclusion of women from military posts, including the use of arms. Women were permitted access only to the medical and military-music services. It held that such exclusion infringed Directive 76/207 and was disproportionate. The exclusion of women from a post was not justified by the directive on the ground that women should be given greater protection than men against risks to which both sexes are equally exposed.

(3) In *Dory v Germany* (Case C-186/01) the ECJ held that Directive 76/207 does not preclude military service being reserved to men.

Equal opportunities and positive discrimination

Key Principle: **Member States may maintain or adopt measures within the meaning of Art.141(4) with a view to ensuring full equality in practice between men and women: Art.2(8) (as amended by Directive 2002/73).**

Kalanke v Frei Hanseatadt Bremen (Case C-450/93) 1995

German Law operated a rule requiring the appointment of the female applicant for a job in the event of applicants being equally qualified in areas where women were under-represented. Mr Kalanke, a landscape gardener with the Bremen Parks Department, claimed that he had been refused promotion in favour of an equally qualified female applicant. The German court made an Art.234 reference to the ECJ.

Held: (ECJ) Art.2(4) of Directive 76/207 (now replaced by Art.2(8)) permits measures giving a specific advantage to women with a view to improving their ability to compete on the labour market and to pursue a career on an equal footing with men. It does not permit "absolute and unconditional priority" to be given to women. [1996] 1 C.M.L.R. 175.

Commentary

(1) The wording of the *Kalanke* ruling found its way into the Treaty via a Social Agreement annexed to the Maastricht Treaty. The ToA incorporated the provision into an amended Art.141 (ex 119) which now reads: "With a view to ensuring full equality between men and women in working life, the principle of equal treatment shall not prevent any member state from maintaining or adopting measures providing for specific advantages in order to make it easier for the under-represented sex to pursue a vocational activity or to prevent of compensate for disadvantage in professional careers". (Note the change from *Kalanke*: the substitution of "under-represented sex" for "women".)

(2) A national rule requiring preference to be given to the promotion of women where there are fewer women than men at the higher level of the relevant post in the public service does not infringe the directive, unless reasons specific to the male candidate tilt the balance in his favour. This exception may only be invoked where there has been an objective assessment of the candidatures which take account of each candidate's specific circumstances: *Marschall v Land Nordrhein Westfalen* (Case C-409/95).

(3) A plan to fill more than half the posts in a sector where women are under-represented by women, either by appointment or promotion, did not infringe the directive, provided it satisfied an objective assessment by the national court in line with *Marschall: Georg Badek* (Case C-158/97).

(4) The ECJ in *Abrahamsson v Fogelqist* (Case C-407/98) interpreted Art.141(4) which allows Member States to take measures for special advantage to ensure full equality between men and women in professional life. The Court held that Directive 76/207 and Art.141(4) preclude national legislation which automatically grants preference to candidates from the under-represented sex, if they are sufficiently qualified, subject only to the proviso that the difference between the merits of the candidates of each sex is not so great as to result in a breach of the requirement of objectivity in making appointments.

Gender reassignment, sexual orientation and equal treatment

Key Principle: **Protection against discrimination on grounds of sex includes the protection of transsexuals.**

P v S (Case C-13/94)
This case involved a claim for unfair dismissal following gender reassignment. (For facts, see Ch.3.)

Held: (ECJ) Discrimination extends beyond the concept of whether an individual is male or female into the area of gender reassignment.

Commentary

(1) *P v S* represents a bold step by the ECJ to extend the concept of discrimination. In the words of Craig & de Burca (in *EU Law: Text, Cases and Materials*, 3rd ed., 2002), "One of the more interesting recent developments in the field of EC law on equal treatment has been the gradual attempt, through litigation, to broaden the concept of sex discrimination beyond the paradigm case of differential treatment of men and women."

(2) The bold step forward did not extend to equal treatment in homosexual relationships. In *Grant v South West Trains* (Case C-249/96) the ECJ held that same sex relationships were not covered by the Equal Treatment Directive. Sexual orientation is however, within the scope of the Directive 2000/78. Grant was followed by the CFI in *D v C* (Case

T-264/97), upheld by the ECJ in Joined Cases C-122/99P and C-125/99P, a staff case, in which the refusal to grant a household allowance to an EC official living with a same sex partner, on the basis that stable relationships between individuals of the same sex could not be equated to marriage.

(3) The two Directives adopted under Art.13 of the Treaty in 2000 amount to a radical departure in terms of scope from previous directives on equal treatment. Directive 2000/43 provides for equal treatment between persons irrespective of racial or ethnic origin. Directive 2000/78 provides a general framework for equal treatment in employment and occupation in order to combat discrimination on grounds of religion or belief, disability, age or sexual orientation. Directive 2002/73 (implementation date October 2005) amended Directive 76/207 so as to bring it in line with Directives 2000/43 and 2000/78. Art.2(3) of Directive 2002/73 prohibits 'harassment' and 'sexual harassment'. Both Directives were due for implementation by July 2003, although the UK was allowed an additional period (up to December 2006) to implement Directive 2000/78.

(4) Directive 2004/114 was adopted in 2004 implementing the principle of equal treatment between men and women in the access of supply of goods and services. It followed a request by the European Council at Nice in December 2000 to the Commission to strengthen equality-related rights in areas other than employment and professional life.

Age discrimination and equal treatment

Key principle: **Non-discrimination on grounds of age is a general principle of Community law.**

Werner Mangold v Rüdiger Helm (Case C-144/04)
A German law adopted in 2000 authorised by conclusion of fixed term contracts of employment once the worker has reached the age of 52, except in specific cases of continuous employment. Mr Mangold, a 56 year old lawyer, entered into contract in Germany by which he was employed by Mr Helm for a fixed period from July 2003 until February 2004. He brought proceedings arising from the contract before the German courts which referred several questions to the ECJ for clarification on the interpretation of Directive 2000/78.

Held (ECJ):   The principle of non-discrimination on grounds of age is a general principle of Community law. The purpose of Directive 2000/78 is to lay down a general framework for certain forms of discrimination, including in particular discrimination on grounds of age, as regards employment and occupation. A difference of treatment on grounds directly of age constitutes direct discrimination prohibited by Community law, unless it is objectively and reasonably justified by a legitimate aim, particularly by legitimate employment policy and labour market objectives. The means to achieve such objectives must be appropriate and necessary.

Commentary

(1) The ECJ recognised that the purpose of the German legislation was to promote the integration into working life of unemployed older workers, in so far as they met difficulties in finding work. While such an objective could be objectively and reasonably justified, the German provision exceeded what was appropriate and necessary to achieve this objective.

(2) While acknowledging that Member States enjoy broad discretion enjoyed in adopting measures to achieve objectives in social and employment policy, the universal application of the national legislation to all workers of 52 and over was seen to have resulted in the exclusion of a significant body of workers from the benefits of stable employment, itself a major element in the protection of workers. In the court's view, the fixing of an age threshold had not been shown to be objectively justified.

Equal treatment in social security

Key Principle: **Men and women should be treated equally in matters of social security: Art.1 of Directive 79/7 on equal treatment in matters of social security.**

Key Principle: **The equal treatment principle applies to the working population, defined as "self-employed persons, workers and self-employed persons whose activity employ-**

ment is interrupted by illness, accident or involuntary unemployment and persons seeking employment (and to retired or
invalided workers and self-employed persons": Art.2 of Directive 79/7.

Drake v Chief Adjudication Officer (Case 150/85) 1986
The applicant gave up her job to care for a disabled mother. An
Art.177 reference was made to clarify the scope of Art.2 of the
Directive.

Held: (ECJ) Art.2 covers all benefits designed to maintain
income where any of the risks specified in the directive have
been incurred. [1986] E.C.R. 1995.

Commentary

(1) Art.3 of the directive (providing that the equal treatment
principle applies to statutory schemes to protect against
sickness, old age, etc., and social assistance schemes set up
to supplement or replace statutory schemes) has been held
to apply to schemes exempting persons of pensionable age
from prescription charges: *R. v Secretary of State for Health,
Ex p. Richardson* (Case C-137/94). Housing benefit was not,
however, covered: *R. v Secretary of State for Social Security,
Ex p. Smithson* (Case C-243/90) because the benefit was not
directly and effectively linked to one of the risks in Art.3(1).
Similar reasoning was employed by the ECJ in *Atkins v
Wrekin District Council* (Case C-228/94) in which a 63-
year-old male was refused public transport concessions,
which were available to women at 60. The concession was
held to be outside Art.3(1), as was a winter fuel scheme for
pensioners: *R. v Secretary of State for Social Security, Ex p.
Taylor* (Case C-382/98).

(2) The equal treatment principle has also been extended to
cover occupational pension schemes (Directive 86/378) and
selfemployment (Directive 86/613). Directive 86/378, currently under review, has largely been superseded by the
Barber decision that pensions paid under occupational pension schemes are "pay" under Art.141 (ex 119): see p.175.

INDEX

LEGAL TAXONOMY

FROM SWEET & MAXWELL

This index has been prepared using Sweet and Maxwell's Legal Taxonomy. Main index entries conform to keywords provided by the Legal Taxonomy except where references to specific documents or non-standard terms (denoted by quotation marks) have been included. These keywords provide a means of identifying similar concepts in other Sweet & Maxwell publications and online services to which keywords from the Legal Taxonomy have been applied. Readers may find some minor differences between terms used in the text and those which appear in the index. Suggestions to *taxonomy@sweetandmaxwell.co.uk.*

(all references are to page number)

ABUSE OF DOMINANT POSITION
  abuse, 159–163
  assessing dominance, 159
  concentrations, 163–167
  dominance, 154–155
  economic strength, 154–255
  general prohibition, 154
  geographical market, 157–158
  market analysis, 159
  mergers, 163
  predatory pricing, 162–163
  product market, 155–157
  refusal to supply, 161–162
ACTIONS FOR ANNULMENT ACTION
  grounds of challenge, 59–62
  locus standi, 53–59
  reviewable acts, 51–53
  right to challenge, 53–59
AGE DISCRIMINATION
  equal treatment, 194–195
AGREEMENTS OF MINOR IMPORTANCE
  anti-competitive practices, 149–150
ANTI-COMPETITIVE PRACTICES
  agreements between undertakings,
    142–143
  comfort letters, 152–153
  concerted practices, 143–144
  distribution agreements, 147–148
  effect on inter-member trade,
    144–145
  "gentlemen's agreement", 142
  illegality, 150–153

ANTI-COMPETITIVE PRACTICES—*cont.*
  market analysis, 147
  minor agreements, 149–150
  prevention, restriction or distortion
    of competition, 145–148
  within the common market,
    148–149
APPRENTICES
  free movement of persons, 119
"APPROPRIATE MEASURES"
  enforcement of EC law, 42
ARCHAEOLOGICAL SITES
  free movement of goods, 100–101
ARMED FORCES
  equal treatment, 191

"BUY BRITISH"
  free movement of goods, 88

CHARGES HAVING EQUIVALENT EFFECT
  free movement of goods, 84–85
COLD CALLING
  freedom to provide services,
    133–134
COMFORT LETTERS
  anti-competitive practices, 152–153
COMMON MARKET
  See SINGLE MARKET
COMMUNITY INSTITUTIONS
  annulment action (Art 230)
    grounds of challenge, 59–62